Theos Friends' Programme

Theos is a religion and society think tank which seeks to inform and influence public opinion about the role of faith and belief in society.

We were launched in November 2006 with the support of the Archbishop of Canterbury, Dr Rowan Williams and the Cardinal Archbishop of Westminster, Cardinal Cormac Murphy-O'Connor.

We provide

- high-quality research, reports and publications;
- an events programme;
- news, information and analysis to media companies, parliamentarians and other opinion formers.

We can only do this with your help!

Theos Friends receive complimentary copies of all Theos publications, invitations to selected events and monthly email bulletins.

Theos Associates receive all the benefits of Friends and in addition are invited to attend an exclusive annual dinner with the Theos Director and team.

If you would like to become a Friend or an Associate, please visit www.theosthinktank.co.uk or detach or photocopy the form below, and send it with a cheque to Theos for the relevant amount. Thank you.

Yes, I would like to help change public opinion!
I enclose a cheque payable to Theos for: ☐ **£60** (Friend) ☐ **£300** (Associate)

☐ Please send me information on how to give by standing order/direct debit

Name _____

Address _____

_____ Postcode _____

Email _____

Tel _____

Data Protection Theos will use your personal data to inform you of its activities.
If you prefer not to receive this information please tick here. ☐

By completing you are consenting to receiving communications by telephone and email. Theos will not pass on your details to any third party.

Please return this form to:
Theos | 77 Great Peter Street | London | SW1P 2EZ
S: 97711 D: 36701

Theos – clear thinking on religion and society

Theos is a Christian think tank working in the area of religion, politics and society. We aim to inform debate around questions of faith and secularism and the related subjects of values and identity. We were launched in November 2006, and our first report *'Doing God'; a Future for Faith in the Public Square,* written by Nick Spencer, examined the reasons why faith will play an increasingly significant role in public life.

what Theos stands for

In our post-secular age, interest in spirituality is increasing across western culture. We believe that it is impossible to understand the modern world without an understanding of religion. We also believe that much of the debate about the role and place of religion has been unnecessarily emotive and ill-informed. We reject the notion of any possible 'neutral' perspective on these issues.

what Theos works on

Theos conducts research, publishes reports and runs debates, seminars and lectures on the intersection of religion, politics and society in the contemporary world. We also provide regular comment for print and broadcast media. Research areas include religion in relation to public services, the constitution, law, the economy, pluralism and education.

what Theos provides

In addition to our independently driven work, Theos provides research, analysis and advice to individuals and organisations across the private, public and not-for-profit sectors. Our unique position within the think tank sector means that we have the capacity to develop proposals that carry values – with an eye to demonstrating what really works.

what Theos believes

Theos was launched with the support of the Archbishop of Canterbury and the Cardinal Archbishop of Westminster, but it is independent of any particular denomination. We are an ecumenical Christian organisation, committed to the belief that religion in general and Christianity in particular has much to offer for the common good of society as a whole. We are committed to the traditional creeds of the Christian faith and draw on social and political thought from a wide range of theological traditions. We also work with many non-Christian and non-religious individuals and organisations.

The future of welfare:
a Theos collection

(ed.) Nick Spencer

Published by Theos in 2014
© Theos

ISBN 978-0-9574743-3-8

Some rights reserved – see copyright licence for details
For further information and subscription details please contact:

Theos
Licence Department
77 Great Peter Street
London
SW1P 2EZ

T 020 7828 7777
E hello@theosthinktank.co.uk
www.theosthinktank.co.uk

contents

contributors		6
foreword	– Rt. Hon. Iain Duncan Smith, Secretary of State for Work and Pensions	7
introduction	– Nick Spencer	9
chapter 1	– falling out of love with welfare – Duncan O'Leary and David Goodhart	17
chapter 2	– the case for connection – Ruth Porter	25
chapter 3	– welfare: some Catholic reflections – Anna Rowlands	33
chapter 4	– welfare, but on what basis? – Christian Guy	43
chapter 5	– the Church of England and welfare today – Malcolm Brown	52
chapter 6	– revisiting Beveridge: principles for affordable, sustainable welfare – Jill Kirby	61
chapter 7	– restoring faith in social security – Stephen Timms	68
chapter 8	– welfare: a Muslim perspective – Shenaz Bunglawala	77
chapter 9	– contract welfare: back to basics – Frank Field	83
chapter 10	– post-liberal politics and the alternative of mutualising social security – John Milbank and Adrian Pabst	90
chapter 11	– between priests and Levites: putting relationship into the heart of the welfare system – Ed Cox	101
chapter 12	– welfare and moral community – Nick Spencer	110
afterword	– Matthew Taylor	118

contributors

Rt. Hon. Iain Duncan Smith is Secretary of State for Work and Pensions

Malcolm Brown is Director of Mission and Public Affairs for the Archbishops' Council of the Church of England.

Shenaz Bunglawala is Head of Research at Engage.

Ed Cox is Director of IPPR North.

Frank Field is MP for Birkenhead.

David Goodhart is Director of Demos.

Christian Guy is Director of the Centre for Social Justice.

Jill Kirby is a freelance writer and policy analyst specialising in social policy, having been Director of the Centre for Policy Studies from 2007-2011.

John Milbank is Professor of Religion, Politics and Ethics at the University of Nottingham, and Director of the university's Centre of Theology and Philosophy.

Duncan O'Leary is Deputy Director of Demos.

Adrian Pabst is Senior Lecturer in Politics at the University of Kent.

Ruth Porter was Communications Director for the Institute of Economic Affairs.

Anna Rowlands is a political theologian and Lecturer in Theology and Ministry at King's College, London.

Nick Spencer is Research Director at Theos.

Matthew Taylor is Chief Executive of the RSA.

Stephen Timms is MP for East Ham.

foreword
Rt. Hon. Iain Duncan Smith, Secretary of State for Work and Pensions

It is a pleasure to preface this collection of essays, which brings together thinkers from across the political arena and beyond, to contemplate the rationale and reason for Britain's welfare state.

Spanning widely divergent ideas about what welfare is, what it should do, and who should provide it, this volume makes for interesting reading. Importantly, it has at its heart a concept of welfare that is far broader than the institution itself. The authors here rightly insist on a moral imperative for welfare, which is, and always has been about people – central to a wider vision of a freer, fairer and more compassionate society, supporting all to live an independent and fulfilling life.

Yet, if this is our ambition for how welfare should work, we must begin by recognising how far the current system has failed in its purpose. Too often, people speak of welfare reform from the standpoint of "I wouldn't start from here" – whether that be means-testing or the contributory principle, reciprocity or redistribution, or another basis for how welfare should work. I believe that is unrealistic; we must start from where we are, rather than where we wish we were.

The reality is that after decades of piecemeal changes, our welfare system has become marred by complexity. There are over 30 different benefits, each with separate rules, some means-tested, others linked, many overlapping. It is a system almost impossible to navigate, except for one thing that is clear: for those entangled in the welfare net, it doesn't pay to work. Thus, even when growth was booming, there were at least four million people on out-of-work benefits. More than a million have ended up stuck there for a decade or more, too many of them unable or unwilling to take the positive step towards self-sufficiency.

There is no kindness in a welfare system which traps the individuals and families it is meant to help, nor anything moral in a fundamentally divided nation, one in which a section of society has been left behind. Yet that is the challenge the coalition government was confronted with on entering office. It has been our starting point, and the reason for taking decisive action to reform the welfare system – a process which is now well under way. In my Department, we are progressing with 45 different projects to restore fairness, integrity and sustainability to our benefit and pension systems. The scale of change is significant. Yet all of these reform programmes are underpinned by a single guiding principle: that everyone in the welfare system should be on a journey, helped and encouraged to move from dependence to independence.

From sickness and disability benefit reform, to Housing Benefit reform and the benefit cap, our aim is to set people on this journey and remove the stumbling blocks in their way. So too through Universal Credit – which has started to roll out this year – merging out-of-work benefits and Tax Credits in order to improve work incentives and restore that seamless process from unemployment to employment. Alongside vital pensions reforms, already introducing automatic enrolment into workplace pensions and bringing in the single tier pension from 2016, we are ensuring that, first it pays to work, and then it pays to save.

These reforms comprise a fundamental shift in Britain's welfare culture, ending the welfare trap and enabling everyone – even those facing the greatest barriers – to make choices that have the potential to transform their lives.

Already we are beginning to see the effects. Employment has increased by over a million people since the election, whilst unemployment has fallen. The UK now has the lowest proportion of workless households since records began, and economic inactivity is at its lowest for two decades. Even in straitened times, we have seen it is possible to make progress towards rebuilding this country's social settlement; restoring fiscal stability, and at the same time restoring lives.

In a time of change, the ideas put forward here are welcome, striking the right balance between support and challenge. Irrespective of their views on the government's position, I would like to thank the contributors. Your voices are testament to the vitality of the current debate, emphasising the significance of welfare as a matter which warrants careful thought. Your essays can only prompt further discussion and deliberation – framing the reforms which I believe are so vital to our welfare state today.

introduction
Nick Spencer

"The time of little adjustments here and there is past; today a radical reconsideration leading to far-reaching changes is inevitable… welfare is in crisis." So wrote the theologian Duncan Forrester in his book *Christianity and the Future of Welfare*, which was published in 1985.

And not just commentators: according to new research undertaken for this collection, nearly nine in ten – 87% – of the British population think that the welfare state is currently "facing severe problems". Over half (58%) think the welfare state is destined to shrink over the next generation and, remarkably, nearly a quarter (24%) think it will no longer be with us in a generation.

Opinions differ by gender, age and class. Women are more pessimistic than men, and people in lower social grades more pessimistic than those in higher ones. Young people are slightly less anxious about its current state and its future: 'only' 75% think it is "facing severe problems", compared with 94% of over-55s. Nevertheless, the sense of gloom, indeed of crisis, is deep and widespread.

Thirty years is a long time to spend on life support and consequently "welfare state in crisis" has become a bit of a truism. At times, the crisis has been downgraded to mere 'unprecedented change'; at others it has been upgraded to a full-blown obituary. Thus, Aditya Chakrabortty writing in the *Guardian* in January 2013, commented that "for much of its short but celebrated life, the Welfare State was cherished by Britons. Instant public affection greeted its birth and even as it passed away peacefully yesterday morning, government ministers swore they would do all they could to keep it alive."[1]

We need to read such hyperbole for what it is. A department with a budget of around £165 billion per year, and national spending that, as a proportion of GDP, has risen from 4.7% in 1951 to 7.2% today hardly marks the grave of the welfare state. The system has always struggled, always evolved, always developed, even during its honeymoon period 60 years ago. Today's system is utterly different from the one Beveridge imagined or Attlee established. Tomorrow's will be different again. The reforms of the present coalition government are indeed serious and significant but they are hardly being conducted on a system that has been held in suspended animation since the last coronation. To borrow from the Protestant reformers, the welfare state is always to be reformed.

The problem with perpetual reform, whether grand-scale or more modest, is that it often limits the opportunities to stand back and ask why. In the words of one of the contributors to this volume, "in all these changes and adjustments through the years, a single, widely supported, narrative about the purposes and principles of a welfare system has been muddled or lost." *The Future of Welfare* is an attempt to regain that narrative or, less grandly, an opportunity for a number of leading thinkers to step back from the policy minutiae and answer the question, 'what is welfare for?' On the premise that if you don't know where you are going you are unlikely to get there, *The Future of Welfare* is an attempt to ask where we are going.

The variety of public diagnoses of the welfare state is testimony to the need to address this 'why' question. A plurality of the public – 32% – think politicians are "mainly to blame" for the welfare state's problems. But, for once, politicians are not simply the scapegoat here and blame is, in fact, apportioned quite widely. A fifth of the public blame mainly "UK benefit claimants, for falsely claiming for benefits", 16% blame "benefits tourists" from other countries, and 15% blame "the European Union, for opening up borders". Tellingly, the only group that is largely exempt is the general public itself, with only 9% of people choosing to blame mainly "British people, for living beyond their means".

In a similar way, there is some disagreement among the general public (and perhaps some confusion) about what welfare is for. On the one hand, 68% of people think that "welfare benefits should be a safety net for only the poorest and neediest in society". On the other, half (50%) agree that "there is no reason why relatively wealthy people should not get some kinds of welfare benefit as long as they have been paying taxes."

In as far as there is a measure of public agreement, it appears to be over the question of who deserves welfare. Around two thirds of people agree that "you should only benefit from state services if you have been paying into the pot which funds them, even if you really need them", whereas only a third agree that "everyone should be eligible to receive welfare benefits, irrespective of whether they have previously paid taxes or not". Many may be uncomfortable with these views, but they appear to indicate the direction of public opinion.

Contributors approach this question from a number of personal and political positions: think tanks and theologians, parliamentarians and policy advisors, left, right and centre. Accordingly, the volume reaches no clear consensus. Then again, none was requested. *The Future of Welfare* was an opportunity for people to think out loud about welfare, without party line, policy details or the pressure for artificial agreement inhibiting them.

The only 'ask' made of the writers was that they think *morally* about the issue, on the basis that, however overgrown it is with fiscal and political concerns, welfare is a fundamentally moral plot. The questions of what are the proper extent and form of our responsibility to one another in this area, and how these should cash out in policy terms, lie only just beneath the surface of the issue.

This is the basis for *Theos'* involvement in the debate. A Christian think tank has no particular wisdom on the details of policy, and welfare can be a bewilderingly detailed policy area. But it does – arguably it must – encourage and engage in the moral debate that underpins those policies. This is what we have attempted in this volume: many contributors (though by no means all) coming from a Christian standpoint, some drawing explicitly on biblical and theological ideas in the process, but all exploring the moral logic of welfare today.

Contributors chose to focus on different aspects of this broad ethical question, but a number of common themes emerged.

One was that of change, already noted. As numerous contributors observed, William Beveridge would hardly recognise the system erected in his name today. Indeed, we would do better to talk about the different British welfare states, than *the* welfare state, as if it were something brought down from Mount Sinai by a great reforming prophet in 1942.

Not surprisingly, therefore, a second emphasis was on the need for ongoing change. Even though different contributors advocated different approaches, none was content with the status quo. They all recognised that the current system faced problems that were more serious – or perhaps more deep rooted – than the obvious economic ones. In particular there were major issues with public opinion (the British appear to have 'fallen out of love with welfare') and with the system's ethical orientation (essays frequently commented on the fact that, with the best will in the world, the current system disincentivised precisely the virtues that society most needed).

If there was some consensus on the nature of the problem, however, there was (a little) less on the solution. This was partly because, as several contributors pointed out, when we talk about welfare we invariably end up talking about much more than welfare. In the words of one essay, "how can we even begin to talk about welfare, without also considering access to education, family breakdown, criminal justice policy, the state of civil society, alcohol and drug addiction, mental and physical health, economic prosperity and the jobs that it creates?" Welfare is complicated because it is about everything. And when people do not agree about everything, it is likely to mean they do not agree about welfare.

That recognised, a number of key ideas for the future of welfare did emerge repeatedly, and they tended to cluster around the idea of *a more relational approach*. If the current system fostered dependency (which is certainly the view of a growing proportion of the population), future reforms needed to emphasise interdependency (none of the essays adopted the libertarian approach of essentially dismantling the entire state welfare edifice in favour of largely unrestrained personal independence). Reciprocity, relationship and mutuality were the watchwords.

Linked to these was the idea that the system needed to ensure people got 'something for something', in the popular political rhetoric of the moment. Reciprocity was a two-way street, in which effort and reward passed one another, and people felt that the system worked for their good rather than in spite of, or even against, it. The future of welfare needed to "embed recipients in relationships of trust and responsibility, with a better balance of entitlements and obligations".

All this pointed in the direction of a contributory system, such as was central to Beveridge's original proposal. However, as several contributors acknowledged, this was a road pitted with problems. Some were economic – where would the money for establishing an insurance-based system come from? – but others were social or moral: what about those people who do not or cannot build up requisite contributions? Would they not lose out in a contributory system? Although a contributory future was the one most frequently cited by writers as best suited to fostering industry and reciprocity, responsibility and 'relationality', it was not an uncomplicated option.

Contributors to *The Future of Welfare* each had around 3,000 words to outline their ideas. The result is a number of very fine, concise, well-informed, and intelligent essays. David Goodhart and Duncan O'Leary from the think tank Demos trace the big shift in the nature of the welfare system, from insurance to redistribution. This, they argue, lies at the heart of national concern about the welfare system, which the public sees as failing to recognise or reward virtuous behaviour, such as work and saving, but it also lies at the heart of the UK system's comparative lack of generosity. The system needs a return to the principle of reciprocity. This, however, would be costly and there is a serious question about how it could be paid for. O'Leary and Goodhart suggest finding the money through reducing other benefits, such as the Support for Mortgage Interest (SMI), as well as targeting some of the existing generous tax breaks for saving that disproportionately benefit the well-off. It is not, they recognise, an easy political option.

Ruth Porter, from the Institute for Economic Affairs, explains Beveridge's original vision and seeks to remake connections that have been severed over the years. She observes that "if state welfare was the answer to meeting needs, poverty rates would be far lower", and argues that prudence should be returned to the heart of welfare. This could be achieved, she argues, through the return to a genuinely contributory system, along with justice and compassion, which require "a free society with minimal coercion". Overall, she contends, we should pay more attention to the processes and values of the system than we presently do.

introduction

Anna Rowlands of King's College, London, uses Catholic Social Teaching for her perspective on the debate. Drawing on four key elements from within this tradition – the understanding of human nature, the role of the state, the obligation to relieve suffering, and the demands of justice – she argues that while the state bears responsibility for the wellbeing of its citizens, that does not mean it is directly responsible for all forms of welfare; it is, to use CST terminology, the instrument of solidarity but not necessarily the substance of that solidarity. Instead of a state that is over- or indeed under-ambitious, we need a genuinely pluralist model, in which state and first-level communities, such as families, faith groups, and local associations, collaborate in pursuit of the Common Good. That emphatically does not let the state off the hook, however, and Rowlands concludes by criticising recent government trends of using welfare privation as a form of social control.

Christian Guy from the Centre for Social Justice argues that it is time for a new social settlement. Vigorously defending the idea and intention of the original welfare settlement, he argues that we need to cast a system which promotes rather than undermines the things which protect against poverty. Any new social settlement demands recognition of the dignity of every human being, and should be "unashamedly focused" on helping people realise their full potential, giving them second chances when the first ones in life fail. That entails focusing on those who need help, rather than designing a system that delivers something for everybody. This means that a re-introduction of a more contributory system is not the panacea some suggest.

Malcolm Brown looks at welfare from the perspective of the Church of England. Contrary to the stereotype, he argues, the church fully recognises the moral vision behind government welfare policy, the reality and problem of welfare dependency, and the perils of a debt economy. But it also has a deep-rooted support for the principle of the modern welfare state, which is more than mere nostalgia, not to mention an authenticity to its analysis, borne of its presence in many of the poorest communities in the country. Recognising that the church is not in a position to offer detailed alternative policy options, Brown nonetheless insists that all reforms must be judged according to the criteria of fairness, generosity, and sustainability. The church can and will continue to provide invaluable welfare services but it cannot simply pick up the responsibility for statutory services.

Jill Kirby, former Director of the Centre for Policy Studies, revisits the original Beveridge report and argues that we find in this the principles of affordable, sustainable welfare. The Beveridge thesis that payments based on contributions improve social cohesion is not only fiscally responsible but ethically sound. There are objections to a contributory system, not least what to do about those who have not contributed but are already in need, but these are not, she contends, insurmountable. By recognising that those who have been unable to make a financial contribution have scope to contribute in other ways; by placing all school and college leavers unable to find work onto a paid work programme, rather than benefits; and by increasing the 'conditionality' tests applied to benefit claimants, a genuine case can be mounted for a reformed, contributory welfare system that encourages rather than undermines individual and family responsibility.

Stephen Timms MP looks to the Bible and the work of faith communities for a new moral foundation for social security. He finds an emphasis on work, on fighting injustice and on hearing the cry of the needy as central to the re-formation of welfare. Not only are faith groups leading the way in terms of providing welfare services and getting people back into employment, but that activity points towards the need to introduce job guarantees and to renew the contributory principle in welfare. Work, responsibility for others and the spirit of reciprocity are, he argues, not simply political necessities but ethical ones too.

Shenaz Bunglawala, Head of Research at Engage, offers a Muslim perspective on the issue, one that is both theologically and sociologically informed. Theologically, she argues that responsibility to the hungry and needy in society is an inextricable part of piety and worship. Sociologically, she writes how the public turn against welfare is often associated with immigration and Islam, which can lead to "the racialisation of 'welfare abusers'". This combination brings her to a powerful defence of the welfare system as encapsulating "the moral injunction to shoulder responsibility for the poor and hungry, the young and the old that Islam commands", a system whose basis of solidarity and empathy should not be eroded by concerns about diversity within society.

Frank Field takes a historical line, tracing the story from the initial intentions of Sidney and Beatrice Webb to establish a national minimum of civilised life, though Beveridge, and then the transformation, effected by Richard Crossman and Barbara Castle, of the original insurance-based model to one based on wage-related benefits which sought to secure greater equality of income over each person's lifetime. This model rapidly proved too expensive, not to mention unpopular. Field argues that we need to reassert the primacy of insurance-based welfare by establishing a new conditional, contract-based welfare model which would realign welfare so that it works with, rather than against, human nature. In effect, this means returning to a system closer, at least in intent, to the Webbs' original vision than what became of that vision in the post-war period.

Adrian Pabst and John Milbank argue against the social and economic liberalism that has dominated post-war Britain, in favour of a more mutualist vision. The welfare settlement, they argue, has tended to function as a substitute for high employment, decent jobs, and widespread asset ownership – the statist model effectively (and ironically) propping up the free market one. In its place, they call for "responsible reciprocity", a mutualised welfare settlement that is personal, local and participatory. This would demand a renewal and extension of Attlee's original idea of a unified insurance-based social security system alongside a 'preferential option for the poor', moving away from means-testing, putting in place what they call a Mutual Jobs Fund, and developing locally-based welfare schemes that embed people in meaningful relationships of reciprocity.

Ed Cox, Director of IPPR North, uses the parable of the Good Samaritan to frame and inform a more relational approach to welfare. Drawing on IPPR research that shows how public understanding of welfare is critical but also badly informed, Cox argues that the rhetorical battle between politicians and media is leading to a race to the bottom in which no-one benefits. Referring to the famous parable from Luke's gospel, he critiques the moral conditionality of right and the bureaucratic conditionality of left, and posits instead a more relational approach to welfare, that is marked by solidarity and empathy, and underpinned by principles of contribution, clarity and co-operation.

Nick Spencer examines the moral centre of gravity of the welfare system in the post-war period, alongside that of the society it serves, arguing that both have changed in such a way as to make the present system unsustainable. The welfare system has changed, he argues, from desert-centred system to a need-centred one just as society has moved from an acute sense of national identity and responsibility to one of pluralism and individualism. A need-centred system, he contends, requires very high levels of responsibility and trust to sustain it and in the absence of these, we face the inevitability of returning to a desert-centred system, based on contribution and insurance.

In his Afterword, Matthew Taylor, Chief Executive of the Royal Society for the Arts, brings the collection down to earth. Recognising that the moral and theological bent of the essays naturally orients them away from practicalities, he nonetheless reminds us that ultimately we need some realism about the nature of practical reform. Reciprocal conditionality might help with incentives, for example, but it probably doesn't help with costs. With this in mind, his brief conclusion outlines three needs – for a concerted attempt at public education; to widen the welfare debate to include all aspects of our society and economy; and to generate cross-party political buy-in for change – if welfare is ever going to be thoroughly and coherently reformed.

Welfare is not a 'problem' to be 'solved', still less solved by a particular department of state or government. Indeed, as Anna Rowlands suggests, it shouldn't perhaps be seen as a problem at all, but rather part of human nature and the calling to bear one another's burdens, as St Paul put it. Precisely which and whose burdens are to be borne and by whom are not questions amenable to solution, but they are amenable to discussion and is our hope that the essays in this volume will make that discussion better informed and more productive.

introduction – references

1. Aditya Chakrabortty, "The Welfare State, 1942-2013, obituary", *The Guardian*, 8 January 2013: http://www.guardian.co.uk/commentisfree/2013/jan/08/welfare-state-1942-2013-obituary.

falling out of love with welfare
Duncan O'Leary and David Goodhart

What we now call 'welfare' was once called 'social insurance.' The change in terminology reflects a shift in the role of the state, away from the practical purposes and moral underpinnings envisaged by its creators.

Today, most of us could describe the essential characteristics of an insurance system. Participants choose to pay into a shared system, allowing risks to be pooled (though those facing bigger risks tend to be required to pay higher premiums). This risk pooling protects individuals against the financial impact of events outside of their control. Payments are made in the event of particular contingencies. Only those who have paid into the system are eligible for payouts. These basic features of insurance help bring "the magic of averages to the benefit of millions", as Winston Churchill once put it.[1]

Churchill was, in fact, describing the social insurance system proposed by William Beveridge. Beveridge's model had three important differences. First, payments would be made at a flat rate into the system, rather than people who faced higher risks paying more. Second, people would have no choice but to buy into the state's social insurance system, with funding drawn through National Insurance. Third, social insurance would be supplemented by social assistance, a means-tested system designed to protect those with nothing from destitution.

Each of these three features was designed to work in the interests of the less well off. The wealthy would be forced to buy the state's insurance 'product', thereby widening the risk pool, while the poor would not be charged higher premiums and would be protected from the worst by the safety net of social assistance.

Despite these aspects, however, Beveridge was determined not to undermine people's capacity for self-help, or the incentive to work. As the introduction to the Beveridge report put it:

> The State in organising security should not stifle incentive, opportunity, responsibility; in establishing a national minimum it should leave room and

> encouragement for voluntary action by each individual to provide more than that minimum for himself and his family.

The report continued:

> It is, first and foremost, a plan of insurance – of giving in return for contributions benefits up to subsistence level, as of right without a means test, so that individuals may build freely upon it.

today's system

Today's system looks very little like the Beveridge model. It remains true that everyone must buy into the system (though through progressive taxation, rather than a flat rate – a change made within a decade of Beveridge's report on affordability grounds) but many of the central tenets of his model have disappeared. The contributory principle has been eroded to a striking degree, with contributory benefits accounting for just 5% of expenditure on working age welfare by 2012.[2]

This has been the result of decisions made by successive governments, from Margaret Thatcher's decision to abolish the Earnings-related Supplement in the early 1980s to the Blair government's expansion of means-tested Tax Credits in the 2000s and the present coalition government's recent decision to time limit contributory entitlements to Employment and Support Allowance. As the contributory system has declined, means-testing has taken over – now accounting for the majority of working age welfare expenditure.

The result of all this has been a fundamental change in the nature of the British welfare system. The balance of welfare has shifted from insurance, towards redistribution. In the words of Tim Horton and James Gregory, this is "a profound change in the relationship between taxpayers and benefit recipients, from one of reciprocity and risk pooling, to one of providing transfers to others on the basis of need."[3]

The practical consequence of this is that Britain now has a welfare system that is good neither at insuring people against loss of income nor at reassuring them that they are not being taken for a ride by others. During the recession, many people were shocked to learn that, despite having worked for many years, they were entitled to just £71.70 per week Job Seekers Allowance. Payments would last for just six months in the case of those with more than £16,000 savings in the bank or a partner in work.

Not only were people surprised at the lack of generosity in Britain's welfare system, many also felt that it was set up to reward the wrong behaviours. Unlike the Beveridge system, those with good work records were entitled to no more than those without a track record of contribution. Further, the means test after six months would punish those who had saved – another behaviour most people believe should be encouraged rather than penalised.[4]

The international evidence suggests this lack of generosity and the absence of a strong contributory principle are linked. Those countries with the weakest contributory elements, such as the UK and New Zealand, also tend to have the least generous entitlements and the most hostile attitudes towards those in receipt of welfare. By contrast, those countries with the strongest contributory elements, such as Austria, Norway and the Netherlands tend to have more generous entitlements and public attitudes. The table below demonstrates this, with countries ranked in order of the percentage of unemployed people receiving contributory benefits.

table 1: contribution, generosity and public support

Country	% unemployed receiving contributory benefits[5]	% unemployed receiving non-contributory benefits[6]	Wage replacement rate %[7]	% agreeing 'Government should provide decent standard of living for unemployed'[8]
Austria	94.1	0.0	55	61.8
Norway	90.0	0.0	64	77.5
Netherlands	67.9	2.3	75	-
Sweden	66.0	0.0	46	77.6
Finland	54.9	11.9	53	80.6
Denmark	53.0	14.4	57	84.3
France	47.9	11.8	66	62.4
Canada	44.4	0.3	62	-
US	37.5	0.0	47	48.6
Germany	30.0	69.0	59	62.3
UK	9.2	42.2	13	53.0
Australia	0.0	68.5	55	52.3
New Zealand	0.0	37.0	26	44.8

The lack of generosity and the weak contributory element of the modern British system combine to convince many people that the system is not really for people like them. The payments are too low to cover many people's living costs in any meaningful way, while the absence of reciprocity leaves people fearful they are subsidising those who choose not to work. Welfare becomes about 'them' not about 'us'. So ingrained is this problem that even those who support the system deploy the hashtag *#HappyToPayYourBenefits* in social media exchanges. There is no sense that people have paid into a system over time and are therefore entitled to support by right, not simply thanks to the generosity of others.

false consciousness

Too often defenders of social security ignore these big shifts in the nature of the welfare system, preferring instead to blame rising public dissatisfaction to a form of false consciousness engendered by politicians and the media. The voters, it is argued, have been 'brainwashed' by unrepresentative anecdotes, inaccurate reporting and clever 'framing' of public debate. These are seductive arguments but not useful ones in explaining the dramatic shift in public attitudes to welfare between the early to mid-1990s and the mid to late 2000s.

In fact, research by Gaffney et al for the charity Turn2Us has found that the number of negative stories about the welfare system actually fell between 1998 and 2003/4 – the period in which support for the welfare system declined on a number of measures. Further, references to 'fraud' in newspaper coverage of welfare declined in number from the late 1990s through to 2009, yet public perceptions of 'fiddling' remained stable rather than falling, in line with the coverage.[9] Similarly, while some argue that the shift in attitudes can be attributed to a toughening of political rhetoric and policy under New Labour – the 'framing' explanation – this is also hard to justify from the evidence.

Though it may be true that most of the decline in support for welfare occurred when Labour was in office, this trend began before Labour won election in 1997 – and potentially before New Labour was even created. Analysis of the British Social Attitudes Survey shows that the proportion of the Labour identifiers picking welfare as one of their top two priorities for extra government spending, for example, peaked in 1989, five years before Tony Blair was elected leader of the opposition and eight years before he became prime minister. Support fell in the majority of the years between 1989 and 1994. Similarly, the proportion of the public agreeing that "the government should spend more money on welfare benefits for the poor, even if it leads to higher taxes" peaked in 1989. Meanwhile, on other BSA questions covering 'fiddling', people 'standing on their own two feet', and the deservingness of recipients, support was already falling by 1994.

None of this is to suggest that media coverage or political rhetoric have no effect on public opinion. Rather it is to recognise that both tend to have a symbiotic relationship with public attitudes, both reflecting and driving opinion. Negative coverage and political rhetoric may therefore have contributed to negative overall attitudes to welfare. But even this interpretation does little to explain the recent swing in attitudes towards a much more negative perception of welfare.

reform

Rather than imagining that the public can be 'framed' and fact checked into changing their minds on welfare, supporters of social security must engage with people's substantive concerns – and the moral position behind them. What people want is not complicated: it is a system that is there for them when they need it and which encourages the right behaviour in others. This implies reforms to the job centres, which people find frustrating and unhelpful, but also to the structure of entitlements.

Almost all of the public concerns about the welfare system – from fears over 'scroungers', to astonishment at the lack of generosity of entitlements, to anger that new migrants might be able to make claims soon after arriving in Britain – stem from a desire for reciprocity. With the decline of the contributory principle, so-called 'conditionality' has had to bear the burden of reassuring people that they were part of a reciprocal system, in which people would work, or at least seek work, in return for making claims. However, terms and conditions alone cannot be enough. The reason for this is that people want to be sure that others have contributed in the past to earn entitlements, or at least will contribute in the future in order to put back into the system.

The table below, taken from research for the Fabian Society[10], illustrates how these perceptions about others' past or future contributions affects people's willingness to commit resources to the welfare system. Those who have the greatest confidence that welfare recipients will work in the future are also those most likely to agree that "the government should spend more on benefits for the poor, even if it leads to higher taxes."

table 2: overall views on welfare spending and benefit recipients[11]

	% Agree	% Disagree	Net agree
The government should spend more on benefits for the poor, even if it leads to higher taxes	24	49	-25
Most people who receive benefits now will make a contribution back to society in the future, through activities like employment or caring for others	25	46	-21
Support for increasing benefits for the poor by views about benefit recipients			
…of those agreeing that most people will make a contribution to society in the future	49	27	+22
…of those disagreeing that most people will make a contribution to society in the future	11	72	-61

contribution

All this points to a return to a system that does more to reward the behaviours that most people want to see in others: work, saving and honesty about financial circumstances. Means-testing can sap incentives for all three of these, while the contributory principle does the opposite. It is the feature of Beveridge's social insurance that must be revised, with higher entitlements reserved for those with good work records.

How to pay for this is the harder part. Finding the money from already low entitlements for non-contributors is an unattractive option; raiding the pensions budget looks unlikely due to fears about 'the grey vote'; asking the public to contribute more in taxation looks politically suicidal. Demos has recommended finding the money through reducing other benefits – specifically Support for Mortgage Interest (SMI) which sees the state pay the interest on people's mortgages when they become unemployed. The case for cutting this benefit is that if people take on the risk of the mortgage then they must also take responsibility for the risk that involves. Savings from SMI could help pay for a two tier system, with higher entitlements for contributors.

Governments should also rethink how to support rather than punish saving, particularly among the low paid. A proper post-mortem is required on policies such as the Savings Gateway and Child Trust Fund, pioneered under the last government but either reformed or scrapped under this one. Funding to back new initiatives in this area could be found by targeting some of the existing generous tax breaks for saving that disproportionately benefit the well off.

These principles ought also to be extended to other aspects of the welfare state. Proposals to means-test pensioner benefits, such as the Winter Fuel Allowance, should be resisted, for example. If savings need to be found then people should simply receive these payments later in life, when fuel poverty is a much bigger risk. This approach would avoid all the bureaucracy and the resentment that comes with means-testing.

In social care, the proposals to cap lifetime care costs have been criticised for the extent to which they will benefitting the middle classes[12] but, in fact, this is the welfare state returning to the idea of social insurance. Risks will be pooled, preventing catastrophic care costs in later life, whilst people will still be expected to display the kind of 'voluntary effort' that Beveridge described in funding or insuring against costs up to the level of the cap. The challenge will be to ensure that the safety net of a means test does discourage people from taking on responsibility where they can.

conclusion

Today's debates over welfare represent a key political battleground and an emotive area of public debate. But beneath the day-to-day skirmishes lie some important philosophical dilemmas about the appropriate balance between competing priorities: universalism versus targeting, contribution versus need; hypothecated funding versus general taxation, public and private insurance. Fundamentally these are each about the state system's core purpose. Should welfare principally be a mechanism for the redistribution of wealth or rather, as Beveridge imagined, a progressive system of social insurance? It is a debate that those who wish to defend social security would do well to engage in, rather than imagine that winning the argument simply requires correcting misinformation and making the case for the current system in more persuasive language.

At heart, what is required is a system with a renewed sense of reciprocity, which does more to reassure people that they will be protected and that other people will contribute. Until governments recommit to this vision, we will go on wondering why the British appear to be falling out of love with welfare.

chapter 1 – references

1   Cited in I Mulheirn and G Masters, *Beveridge Rebooted*, Social Market Foundation (2013).
2   P Wintour, "Ed Miliband faces a stiff test over welfare policy", *Guardian*, 5 June 2013.
3   T Horton, J Gregory, *The Solidarity Society*, Fabian Society (2009).
4   B Duffy, S Hall, D O'Leary, S Pope, *Generation Strains*, Demos (2013).
5   K Bell, D Gaffney, *Making a Contribution*, TUC (2012).
6   K Bell, D Gaffney, *Making a Contribution*, TUC (2012).
7   http://www.oecd.org/els/benefitsandwagesstatistics.htm, Net Replacement Rate for single, childless couples.
8   Gesis, "International Social Survey Programme: Social Inequality IV – ISSP 2009".
9   Baumberg et al, Benefits Stigma in Britain, Turn2Us, http://www.turn2us.org.uk/PDF/Benefits%20Stigma%20in%20Britain.pdf.
10 T Horton, J Gregory, *The Solidarity Society*, Fabian Society (2009).
11 T Horton, J Gregory, *The Solidarity Society*, Fabian Society (2009).
12 "Extra cash for social care should be targeted at poorest old people, warns major think tank", press release, Centre for Social Justice, 19 May 2012.

the case for connection
Ruth Porter

In 2013 Mick Philpott was sentenced to life imprisonment for the horrendous deaths of his six children. The Philpott family were receiving close to £60,000 a year in benefits. The media dragged the story into a discussion about whether this was reasonable. The question was how can a system enable people to live as these people had been living? Face-to-face with media pundits like Owen Jones, from the *Independent*, I got dragged into a media storm debating the merits of our welfare system while contemplating the horrors those children had faced.

Within days I found myself back in a studio on the same topic; this time for ITV's *Daybreak* programme, listening to a lady who had spent her whole life living on benefits. Her suggestion that living on welfare was a lifestyle choice so outraged viewers that the item was written up by the *Daily Mail*. They quoted the lady saying:

> I get £142 a fortnight. I buy my cigarettes, a drink at weekends, shopping, and various things to economise. I think it's outrageous [to suggest we change spending habits]. I wouldn't want to stop doing anything really, it's the way I've been brought up – to spend my benefits on what I'm used to, to survive.

The *Daily Mail* then wrote up her next comment, explaining:

> Asked what she would say to people who have jobs and work long hours but still can't afford luxuries, Tracey, from Manchester replied: 'Well that's their choice isn't it? Like it's our choice to do what we're doing.'[1]

What those media debates and the appetite for them shows, is that the public intuitively knows that something has gone badly wrong with our welfare system. Neither of these cases was in any way typical of how people on welfare live, yet somehow they have become linked in the public consciousness to what living on welfare can do to people. The current incentives in the system can be demotivating, destructive and can undermine people's ability to take responsibility for themselves and their families. The system has been distorted into something far removed from what Beveridge had originally intended – a form of savings to fall back on in times of difficulty and a lifeline to those in desperate need.

The difficulty with debating welfare in these formats is that the pattern of welfare in the UK is hugely complex and subtle, and the struggles people face even more intricate and mired in challenge. An eight-minute head-to-head broadcast debate on welfare will never solve the issue, but it can at least raise an important question. How can we even begin to talk about welfare, without also considering access to education, family breakdown, criminal justice policy, the state of civil society, alcohol and drug addiction, mental and physical health, economic prosperity and the jobs that it creates?

Yet this is precisely what we have done with our modern welfare system. We have assumed that people are simple enough to be reduced to a few tick boxes on a form and that a uniform one-size-fits-all grid of provision across the whole country is the best way of meeting need.

The Christian faith should leave us feeling acutely that something is not right with the system. We have stripped people of part of their dignity, forcing them to look first to the state before looking to those around them. Since when did building a society become about removing the value of relationships and replacing them with a cheque? We have allowed a narrative to grow that ignores the rich diversity of people and their circumstances.

Since its inception the church has taught that human flourishing is not just about survival or the meeting of material needs. This is borne out by wrenchingly sad research showing how lonely and isolated so many feel in Britain today. It is established through the empirical link of work to happiness. But, more than this, it is obvious from the plethora of government- and council-provided services up and down the country that fail to take hold – youth clubs on impoverished estates or vans for those selling sex on the streets. Time and time again, it is the services run by charities that are effective, not those propagated by bureaucracy. Why should anyone be surprised? In New Zealand, I helped vulnerable refugees who had fled desperate conditions in the Congo. I saw repeatedly how they turned to volunteers over social workers when placing their trust. Knowing that people's agenda was simply to care for them and help them as they started a new life carried immense power. Social workers may have had greater expertise and an important role to play, but the fact they were being paid to do a job meant their help could only ever go so far.

The replacement of people by systems has been the subject of science fiction and political novels for years. Perhaps the reason we fear so much their dehumanising consequences is because if we do not have the freedom to act how can we be responsible? How can we be moral? As the philosopher John Stuart Mill said, if we surrender too much to the state we risk losing something of ourselves: "A people among whom there is no habit of spontaneous action for a collective interest – who look habitually to their government to command or prompt them in all matters of joint concern – who expect to have everything done for them… – have their faculties only half developed."[2] The dominance of the state in our lives is a relatively new phenomenon in Britain and was not the original intention when the modern welfare system was established.

what was Beveridge trying to do?

In 1942, William Beveridge published his plan for improving financial provision for people in difficult times. The plan covered a pension in old age, medical treatment, funeral expenses, provision in case of unemployment or disability, and maternity cover.

Underpinning the desire to shift responsibility for administration of a national insurance system to the state were two ideas: a belief that by virtue of a shared nationhood people had a moral duty to one another; and that due to various factors including insufficient contributions being made, current insurance systems were not providing adequate cover.

Beveridge's aim was social progress. And he saw the development of his system as one small part of achieving it. He argued that "social insurance fully developed may provide income security; it is an attack upon Want. But Want is one only of five giants on the road to reconstruction and in some ways easiest to attack. The others are Disease, Ignorance, Squalor and Idleness."[3]

Although he valued the certainty that he believed a national scheme would bring, he was cautious about ensuring that the moral and social fabric that made up society wasn't damaged:

> The State in organising security should not stifle incentive, opportunity, responsibility; in establishing a national minimum, it should leave room and encouragement for voluntary action by each individual to provide more than that minimum for himself and family.[4]

In considering the different options of state provision or facilitation, Beveridge opted for a compulsory insurance, rather than means-testing. Interestingly, he argued that the general public preferred a contributory system. One of the reasons he credited for this was their affection for prudence. "This objection [to means-testing] springs not so much from a desire to get everything for nothing, as from resentment at a provision which appears to penalise what people have come to regard as the duty and pleasure of thrift, of putting pennies away for a rainy day."[5]

Much of his motivation and concern hinged on a Christian ethic – he saw the desperate need to help those in times of trouble, but felt keenly the desire to ensure the human face of charity was preserved. He also valued the personal development of character, through exercising prudence and thrift.

what kind of Britain has our welfare system built?

The welfare state today is far removed from that originally intended. The connection between contribution and receipt has been eroded and the expectations of what the state will provide have expanded to take in areas such as social care funding.

In the UK, around 40% of government spending is now on welfare, with a substantial proportion of all welfare spending now on state pensions. In order to fund this spending we have burdened Britain with so much debt we now spend nearly as much on interest repayments as we do on education. This high spending has also stripped the economy of investment and space for the private sector, hampering growth and job creation. Even more worrying from a moral perspective is the implicit obligation it has placed on future generations.

That is just the economics of it, though, and whilst that might be one catalyst for change, the human cost of the culture that welfare dependency creates is much higher. Public opinion is shifting markedly on welfare provision. One of the most popular policies any party has pursued in a long time is the welfare cap. Strikingly many people feel this doesn't go far enough. A recent YouGov poll found that:

> Nearly one in five would cap the benefits available at £26,000 – the average earnings of a British family after tax – while only around one in 10 says that there shouldn't be a maximum amount that a family can receive. Moreover, over two thirds of the British public thinks that benefits for a family should be capped at under £20,000 a year after tax, regardless of the number of dependents.[6]

With the high cost of living, created in part by government regulation and subsidies distorting the market in energy, housing, childcare and food, among others, the scope of the welfare state has also broadened and is now acting as a top-up to many people's income.

The effective marginal tax rates (i.e. the combined effect of tax and benefits) created by the withdrawal levels of benefits combined with other taxes are high and can therefore discourage work. The introduction of Universal Credit – the single, means-tested welfare benefit which is replacing the range of previous benefits, such as Jobseeker's Allowance, Employment and Support Allowance, Income Support, Working Tax Credits, and Housing

Benefit – may make some small difference here, but the problem will still remain, with an implicit marginal tax rate of 76%.

There are broadly four groups who are in receipt of benefits today:

- older people through the state pension, pension credits and non-means-tested benefits such as Winter Fuel Allowance;
- the unemployed who want to find work and are unable to do so, and those who don't try to find work;
- those in work who are struggling because of the high cost of living;
- people who need short-term or long-term help through ill health.

This is a massively expanded reach to that originally intended and the moral obligations in each area will be different.

what should be at the heart of welfare?

Prudence

At the very heart of morality is the question of responsibility, for ourselves as well as for others.

For most of the people under the shadow of the welfare system described previously, a return to a genuinely contributory system would enshrine responsibility at the core of the welfare system. People could pay in an insurance contribution that would pay out in times of need caused by unemployment or old age. This would be a transactional arrangement and the central moral element of prudence would be fostered.

The moral question of welfare goes beyond providing for oneself, however, and extends to where our moral responsibility for others lies.

There is a balance to be struck about to the extent to which care, both financial and other, is provided by the state or by individuals, families and civil society. Stacking the balance heavily towards the state has been a relatively recent development. The idea of entitlement and a focus on rights has centralised welfare provision and expanded it, along with increasing dramatically the tax take required to fund it. This is not a development we should welcome. If state welfare was the answer to meeting needs, poverty rates would be far lower.

Justice and compassion

When it comes to the financing of welfare it is worth remembering that if an act is coerced it has a different type of moral worth to an action that is voluntary. If I give £50 to my neighbour who can't afford to buy food for their family that week, that has a different moral worth to the action of the state taking £50 from me and giving it to that neighbour.

Entrenched and expansive welfare states can create a form of spiritual or social poverty by crowding out values such as self-esteem, self-discipline and other attributes crucial to fostering responsibility. In a paper published by the Institute of Economic Affairs, Nima Sanandaji examined how welfare had undermined important social norms and moral virtue in Sweden:

> As Swedes became accustomed to a system of high taxes and generous government benefits, the norms gradually declined. In the World Value Survey of 1981-84, almost 82% of Swedes agreed with the statement, 'claiming government benefits to which you are not entitled is never justifiable.' Sweden was still a nation with very strong morals related to public benefits. As the population adjusted its norms to the higher tax regime, the number who held this view dropped steadily in further surveys. In the survey of 1999-2004, only 55% of Swedish respondents believed that it was never right to claim benefits to which they were not entitled.[7]

In his encyclical letter, *Deus Caritas Est*, Pope Benedict XVI looked at the moral obligation of people to justice as well as charity. We have a duty to help ensure that systems are fair and will create the conditions for people to flourish in. But for too long there has been an assumption that just systems are those based on redistribution and statism. Building a society where jobs are created, diverse education exists and strong families are maintained is at the heart of real justice.

The political thinker David Green has examined the rationales for different societal structures, and gets to the heart of why a free society with minimal coercion is crucial to meet the obligations of morality. "In a civil association [people] are expected to develop their character, to think and judge and to live their lives as a struggle to be better people."[8]

Pope Benedict XVI goes further, explaining why our moral duties cannot simply be absolved by abdicating them to the state:

> There is no ordering of the State so just that it can eliminate the need for a service of love. Whoever wants to eliminate love is preparing to eliminate man as such. There will always be suffering which cries out for consolation and help. There

will always be loneliness. There will always be situations of material need where help in the form of concrete love of neighbour is indispensable. The State which would provide everything, absorbing everything into itself, would ultimately become a mere bureaucracy incapable of guaranteeing the very thing which the suffering person – every person – needs: namely, loving personal concern. We do not need a State which regulates and controls everything, but a State which, in accordance with the principle of subsidiarity, generously acknowledges and supports initiatives arising from the different social forces and combines spontaneity with closeness to those in need.

Intrinsic value vs. outcome

When it comes to welfare we tend to focus on the outcomes. It was this, after all, that drove Beveridge to set up his scheme in the first place. But over the long term, outcomes are shaped by the small decisions, the process. It is the intent behind the act which drives and shapes its morality. As people; we are driven by incentives and prejudices and formed by social bonds and norms. The problem with the system that tries to focus on outcomes, and especially on equal outcomes, as our current welfare system does, is that it removes any connection between action and consequence. In doing so, it destroys the very reflex which encourages moral action. By consequence, this breeds a sense of entitlement. This undermines social bonds both in families and also communities more broadly.

an uncomfortable truth

We have a built a system far removed from the ethical base it was originally designed around, but also one that is distant from any desirable moral framework. It is a convenient system. It is the kind of system a moral reformer like Charles Dickens would have parodied. Contracting out welfare is comfortable in a world where we often feel we lack the time or inclination to volunteer, to bother to get to know our neighbours or even to visit family members. We have an entirely impersonal system that centres on providing money with no investigation into personal circumstances and no discretion.

There are no easy answers for how we reform it. Our lives have grown around the system and change must be gentle. But if we want to meet more of the suffering we see in this country, reform it we must. A greater emphasis on the contributory principle – returning much of the provision to an insurance system – would be a start. But we must go further and consider not just how to foster individual responsibility but also social bonds, and what can be done to strengthen family, community and charity. Here lies the hope of a better system.

chapter 2 – references

1. *Daily Mail* 21 March 2013 http://www.dailymail.co.uk/news/article-2296893/Welfare-mother-Tracey-MacDonald-defends-right-buy-booze-cigarettes-ITVs-Daybreak.html#ixzz2cJxo2YRr.
2. J. S. Mill, *Principles of Political Economy* (Prometheus Books, USA: 2004), p. 863.
3. W. Beveridge, *Social Insurance and Allied Services* (HM Stationery Office, UK: 1942).
4. W. Beveridge, *Social Insurance and Allied Services* (HM Stationery Office, UK: 1942).
5. W. Beveridge, *Social Insurance and Allied Services* (HM Stationery Office, UK: 1942).
6. http://yougov.co.uk/news/2012/01/21/benefits-cap-proposal/
7. N Sanandaji, *The surprising ingredients of Swedish success – free markets and social cohesion*, (Institute of Economic Affairs, 2012).
8. D. G Green, *From Welfare State to Civil Society* (NZBRT, 1996), p. 28.

welfare: some Catholic reflections
Anna Rowlands

rethinking the consensus

Ensuring that all citizens within a nation state are protected from destitution and receive basic care and subsistence when in need is typically seen as the basic purpose and core characteristic of the welfare state. Understanding why such protection is due and the form it should take has varied very significantly both within Europe and beyond.

Here I will address a Catholic perspective on these questions. I should stress that this is *a,* and not *the* Catholic perspective, but it is drawn from my reading of the tradition of Catholic Social Teaching. This tradition began formally in 1891 with an attempt to link classic Christian teaching on justice, virtue and the Kingdom of God, pioneering practices of Christian social care, and the social and economic upheavals of the industrial revolution.

To date, a dozen social encyclicals have been produced to reflect on 'the social question'. I draw from this tradition for two reasons: firstly, because this is where Catholics would turn in order to reflect on what their tradition teaches about the welfare state, and secondly for more historical reasons: because Catholic social doctrine has been a mainstay of influence within and beyond Christian Democracy in the shaping of 19th and 20th century views of the 'why' of welfare and the practice of the 'how' of welfare.

a positive vision of welfare

Whilst the welfare state is often assumed to have strong ties to basic Christian morality, in fact the fundamental connections between the modern welfare state and Christian theology have never been fully worked through. Therefore, the resources for rethinking the relationship between Christianity and the welfare state cannot simply be reached down from the shelf, dusted off and checked for contemporary relevance. Indeed, forging the connections between the two may challenge the assumptions of both left and right on faith and welfare.

Sources for this wider analysis are found in scriptural and doctrinal views of a) basic Christian anthropology: views of what it means to be human in light of our creation in the divine image; b) reflections on the purpose and ends of human community: particularly the nature and duty of the state; c) direct biblical teaching on the obligation to care for those suffering or in social or economic need, in addition to accumulated Christian wisdom on the social practice of care; and d) Christian philosophical and theological concepts of justice.

As bearers of God's image we are understood to mirror in our nature the orientation towards community and relationship that exists within the godhead. We are made for friendship, participation and for a degree of interdependence. As those made in God's likeness, we are imbued with an inalienable dignity that should be supported both by the way we live our own lives as persons in community and the way in which the community, through law and social justice, makes the living of those lives possible. Scripture tells us that to seek our own welfare, the welfare of our neighbour and the welfare of the city is core to our purpose and our nature, and is connected to our salvation. For Christians there is a basic and fundamental connection between welfare and redemption. Therefore, and fairly counter-culturally at the moment, Catholic talk of 'welfare' in its most general sense does not start from a place of lack or negativity, nor of naïve paternalism, but instead has positive connotations derived from our orientation towards the common good – in its transcendent and immanent dimensions.

It is as a result of this profoundly social worldview that both Catholic and Anglican traditions have stressed that poverty matters for reasons of *moral* and *spiritual* welfare, as well as for more immediate physical and material ones. Poverty prevents crucial forms of social participation through enforcing isolation and therefore frustrates the development of capability, character and human flourishing. Poverty in all its forms matters not just for the human economy but also within the economy of salvation. Therefore, from a Christian point of view, the question of welfare can never be considered 'merely' political. Expressed differently, the theological is always necessarily political and the political always theological.

the moral vision of the state

This basic thinking about our nature is mirrored by analogy in the way Catholics view the purpose of the state and its role. Anglican Archbishop William Temple's coining of the phrase 'welfare state' dates from around 1928. His use of the phrase did not in fact directly refer to the kind of state-coordinated social welfare programmes that we now associate with this term. Instead, when he spoke of 'the welfare state' he was referring to the general orientation of a Christian state in all its actions towards providing a synthesis of order for the national community. Thus a 'welfare state' was not a power state that ruled over its communities, but a state that saw itself as an organ of that community. What Temple aimed to capture was a matter of orientation, self-understanding and character within the modern state. A welfare state is an active state oriented towards much more than just law and order and civil liberty: it also offers co-ordinating provision for the economic, social and cultural needs of the wider community.

Similar thinking is also found in CST. The moral purpose of the state is found in its duty to seek the welfare of its members, and in turn, to act in its own inter-state relations in such a way that it helps its members balance their domestic and overseas duties towards the welfare of others. Being a 'welfare state' in this more general sense implies mediating relationships *external* as well as *internal* to national boundaries. We are not used to thinking now in such terms.

The 'internal' duties of the state with regard to welfare include the task of ensuring laws and institutions and the 'general character of administration' in a political community should be such that they 'help realise public well-being'. Whether a state is truly a welfare state relates to the manner in which the state conducts itself across its institutional life: again, it is a matter of *character*. CST, committed to the wider political role of the community as a whole, and a priority for the family and a healthy associational approach, is clear that the state is to be the *instrument* of solidarity, but crucially *not* necessarily always the *substance* of that solidarity.

The substance of solidarity – including key elements of welfare provision – belongs predominantly amongst first-level communities: families, households, faith groups, local associations, and so forth. CST has often in this light been presented as more cautious and suspicious of the powers and role of the state, driving a tendency in some European Catholic countries towards a priority for family-based welfare and a suspicion of state-based welfare. Such interpretation represents a partial truth. Certainly CST does not think that the State alone should provide for welfare through impersonal programmes or structural solidarity. It has always been suspicious of this.

However, CST does have rather more to say about what the state *should* do than we've tended to notice. CST comments on two paradoxical temptations to which the state is always subject: the first is *under-ambition* on the part of the state, in which government perceives its role in a minimalist manner and thus fails to extend itself fully in the search for the common good; the second is *over-ambition* in which the state assumes unto itself all forms of political and social function, failing to perceive the distinction between being an instrument and being the sole substance of social solidarity.

welfare economics

Most of the 'sins' of the state in relation to welfare fall somewhere between these two. A bloated state that thinks all welfare functions happen under its auspices quickly becomes inefficient and ineffective, thus rendering it unable to carry out its true functions. A bloated state also tends to strip middle level associations of their role, and thus feeds a tendency to narrow politics to the work of government alone, which undermines liberal democracy itself. It is one of the state's self-harming instincts. CST also observes that an inefficient and overburdened state is ironically more likely to become slave rather than master of economic forces.

Being a mediating master rather than slave of economic forces is basic to CST's understanding of the welfare role of the state. CST suggests that the state bears responsibility for ensuring the wellbeing of its citizens in the context of the inevitable and problematic fluctuations of capitalism. Markets cannot be left simply to regulate themselves, because capitalism cannot guarantee human dignity.

Within the current economic system, CST thus proposes a moral priority be made by the state for directing practical welfare support towards workers and their dependents, those unable to work within the labour market, and the poor.[1] This does not amount to a vast version of an individual state compensation scheme. Rather, it envisages a combination of redistribution, risk management, social enterprise, and individual support as part of a series of wider structural interventions that seek to manage the 'welfare' duty of the state at a micro and macro-strategic level.

CST refuses to divorce a conversation about structural change from one about what is due directly to the individual from the state. This implies a comprehensive public economic policy that maximises the potential for employment and enterprise within a healthy economy, as well as providing mediating structures that minimise the impact of inevitable instability on workers, their families and 'the poor'. CST also insists that not everyone will be able to participate in a system in which all value is derived from participation in a labour market. Human dignity is rooted in social relations prior to and in excess of the labour market. This has consequences for the provision of welfare.

In relation to workers, basic social insurance, pension, sickness protection and appropriate legal measures to maximise safety in the working environment are all suggested. The state should work in partnership with employers to ensure all workers have access to a 'living wage', and the criteria for judging this is set out by Pope John XXIII in *Gaudium et Spes* and John Paul II in *Laborem Exercens*.[2] For those unable to work or without work, the state must ensure the provision of a minimum income, provision for healthcare, and education as well as access to the basic services necessary for social participation.

This emphasis on social justice – maximising opportunities for continued social participation – is one of the core distinctive features of CST. This is rooted, as suggested above, not just in a view that poverty threatens physical wellbeing but also that poverty breeds isolation, and therefore is a fundamental distortion of the core of our purpose and nature. In this context, welfare provision should be measured against relative and absolute standards: the level of provision necessary to ensure not simply survival but social, political and economic participation within a particular cultural context.

We might note that these conditions for participation may well vary both *between* nations: Britain and Singapore, France and Nigeria; but also *within* a given national context: London to Hull, urban to rural. In the context of the rapid growth of benefit dependency amongst the in work poor, as well as the growth of radical employment instability represented by zero-hour contracts, CST would, I think, view these economic realities as profound *welfare* questions.

Such questions find their structural elements in the call CST makes for living wages as morally preferable to in-work benefit subsidy or insecure contracts, in ways of stabilising employment through worker representation in governance and a greater partnership between labour and capital in the development of creative ways of providing stability within economic life. A true 'welfare state', therefore, pays greater attention to the relationship *between* housing, healthcare, education, business and enterprise, and welfare policy and looks at maximising social participation in finding creative solutions to contemporary problems.

welfare society

Whilst Catholic Social Teaching places a strong emphasis on the moral duties of the state, it might better be said to be concerned with fostering the growth of a plural *welfare society* rather than a just a welfare state. This isn't because of what Catholics are *against*, it is more about what they are *for*: a recognition that the common good cannot be achieved by the state alone and requires wide participation at all levels of society.

This view is reinforced through its emphasis on the relationship between solidarity and subsidiarity. Subsidiarity concerns the best way in which aid or helping assistance can be provided. CST proposes that solidarity is increased when it operates at a level closest to those requiring assistance, at a subsidiary level.

These principles are complemented by a further CST emphasis on social justice; the common good, participation and subsidiarity are seen in the context of the reality of radical inequality of power. Addressing this, the 1931 encyclical *Quadrogesimo Anno* insists that policy makers must maximise participation of those with least direct economic and political power through finding ways to ensure their voices are heard at the forefront of policy debates and formation. For these reasons CST rejects *solely* statist solutions to the provision of welfare in favour of a belief that social care and provision of welfare happen in a more dignified and efficient way when they can be personalised and tailored to the needs they serve. That recognised, the state still remains fundamental as an instrument of this task. This approach lies between the radically corporatist and the primarily statist: it is a *pluralist* model which proposes a wide social collaboration in building a welfare society, with the state continuing to bear responsibility for some aspects of welfare delivery and its coordination but accepting that a diversity of partnership will be core to its dignified, efficient and socially creative practice.

ideas of justice

Many of these ideas about welfare are derived from the Aristotelian-Thomist theory of justice as distributive, contributive and commutative. Firstly, justice is concerned with the meeting of basic needs and the fair or just distribution of resources – including the fair distribution of justice itself.

Secondly, justice also has a contributive character: this implies a) a duty to contribute actively to the system of which I am part, and b) in order to make my contribution I must have real freedom to shape the laws to which I will be subject. A crucial part of the contributive character of justice is, therefore, my freedom and duty to contribute to the common good and to shape the laws to which I will be subject, and my willingness to work actively to contribute to my society.

Less commonly spoken of these days is the notion of justice as 'commutative'. This refers simply to justice as a form of person-to-person conduct, much of which falls outside of 'the law' and concerns the charitable and personal contractual relationships of trust and humanity we form between ourselves. It is through *interpersonal* relationships that justice and charity meet.

It is, of course, noteworthy that many Conservative and Labour politicians believe there to have been an overemphasis on the distributive character of welfare and insufficient on the contributive function. This is perceived to have led to a breakdown in the necessarily reciprocal character of a healthy welfare exchange. Policy discussion has moved to consider examples, like Workfare, that value the contributory principle.

In formal terms, CST would welcome some re-balancing of discussion about welfare towards the threefold characteristics of a just exchange. However, it might offer the following points for consideration. Firstly, the contributory principle is rooted in freely given action that can be exhorted but perhaps not so easily coerced, without risking changing its character. Catholic understandings of the contributory principle are rooted in a theology of gift and of virtue, not in a narrow and punitive understanding that 'you can only take out what you've put in'. Responsibility is thought about always in the context of gratuitousness.

As a practical illustration, CST recognises that life in a volatile market economy produces periods in which low employment and or predominantly low wage economics may mean it is virtually impossible to have made your contribution to the system before you 'take out': here such provision becomes part of the basic conditions for the continued social participation of those without work during such periods, and the need for greater state welfare ought to be raising wider questions about the moral performance of the economy.

The challenge is thus to generate social, political and economic structures that promote (and where necessary, provide) welfare which has as its goal both basic material subsistence, and helps structure self interest towards active social, political and economic participation. Compulsory contributory practices and policy that enable only those who have 'put in' to 'take out' risk producing self-defeating public policy, no matter how superficially popular they may appear in polling data and focus groups.

Secondly, the contributory principle is not a self-standing principle. It works to realise justice when the commutative and redistributive characteristics are also honoured. Thus, the emphasis on contribution may be welcomed, but attention to its *form* remains critical, including attention to how all three elements of just conduct might be balanced in public policy. State welfare is emptied of character or value not only when it ceases to be a 'reciprocal' exchange – a personal transaction – but also when its core morality is derived from a narrow social contract that works only according to logic of calculation and cannot accommodate a logic of gift.

the uses and abuses of welfare privation

One example of the failure to balance such criteria might be found in an area of policy evolution that has produced surprisingly little discussion: the move towards the introduction of privative welfare policy, one intended to cause a degree of privation. Such policy aims to change social behaviour through structures of welfare policy, primarily by limiting or removing support from vulnerable groups. Such initiatives began first amongst non-citizen groups and have included the setting of support levels for migrants at below subsistence levels, the refusal of work to long term migrants awaiting the administration of their application, and the withdrawal of support for those who have exhausted their appeal rights. In the first instance, such policy has been used both to incentivise migrants to transit elsewhere and those without status to return 'home' (self-deportation).

However, as leading judge Stephen Sedley has pointed out, the withdrawal or minimising of support for those in the UK to a level which *maintains or causes* deprivation is being used as the front line of an immigration deterrence policy: to create a hostile welfare environment through which other potential migrants will be deterred from seeking entry. An enforcement first policy fails to identify the earlier failures in the immigration system that might leave migrants in limbo and risks firstly, further reinforcing the entrapment of migrants in spirals of exclusion; and secondly, failing to use the law and public policy to deal with the individual person in community. In cases where the judicial process seems to have failed, migrants find that ironically the final line of border enforcement comes from the *welfare* state.

This seems an extraordinary shift in character and intention with regard to the social use of welfare and has happened gradually. In the absence of any sustained objection to its use in the case of non-citizens, we are now extending such enforcement and social control measures, deployed through the mechanisms of the welfare state, to British citizens. Examples of privative policies include the use of welfare penalties for numbers of children born to those receiving welfare and for those who fall under the terms of the so-called 'Bedroom Tax'.

Of all the proposed and recent changes, this creeping practice of welfare privation as a form of social control – a weapon in the state's arsenal – seems both the most incontrovertibly antithetical to the spirit and letter of CST, and a shift in the fundamental character of European welfare states. Here the intervention of the state cannot be judged as alleviating suffering, managing risk or enabling participation. Rather, the state as agent risks intensifying the suffering of those with least capacity to shape the laws to which they are subject. These are not the conditions in which virtue flourishes. Moreover, a theological argument can be made that the state is both overreaching its own function and distorting its own character through such uses of the welfare system.

concluding thoughts

Of course, an essay on the 'why' of welfare and one which draws from a tradition of political thought (CST) that deliberately stops short of recommending concrete policy practice, leaves out the really challenging part of the conversation. This is the meat of the common good process: a lively and truly contributive process in which we thrash out the shape of a sustainable and practical welfare policy and practice. Amongst other things, that would require us to talk more about the moral basis of the taxation that largely funds the welfare state, and what it means to be a stake holder in our current economy and society. What I have hinted at above is simply some limited resources to aid that conversation. The goal of a welfare system is ultimately a positive one within a broken reality, and its positive ambitions can be framed thus: how can the state and the plural organs of civil society maximise the social, economic and political participation of all its members (including its temporary members) and exercise a duty of care towards its most vulnerable?

There are two forms of inevitable moral tensions in translating the reflections above into practical policy: Christian theology calls us to recognise the infinite character of giving in charity and justice, whilst public policy decisions are made on the basis of the finite, precarious character of material goods and resources. Secondly, we will inevitably disagree on our answers to this question (indeed, possibly on the framing of the question itself!). The question then becomes: what kind of public negotiation can take place as we negotiate the creative tensions of the common good? And to this CST adds one important twist: *who* will participate in that conversation?

chapter 3 – references

1   It is important to note however, that one weakness is that CST has tended to think of workers as primarily male breadwinners and it continues to present an ambivalent account of women as workers. This is an area for particular attention given the gendered characteristics of contemporary labour markets.

2   See *GaudiumetSpes*, paragraph 67; *LaboremExercens*, paragraphs 16 and 17.

welfare, but on what basis?
Christian Guy

the right questions

It is perhaps inevitable, during a period of prolonged austerity, that welfare policy has been one of the most fiercely contested battlegrounds in British politics. UK plc is forecast to spend £210.5 billion on social security and Tax Credits alone in 2013/14, which represents nearly a third of the £720 billion the government will spend during the financial year.[1] Over the course of the 2010/15 parliamentary term, even after well-documented fiscal constraint the coalition has set in train, the UK's social security bill (including Tax Credits) will amount to more than £1 trillion.

Too often the debate about welfare reform, under this government and its predecessors, has been conducted through the narrow lens of spending. This failure to ask the wider foundation questions about our welfare system is understandable in the cut and thrust of political life – both for oppositions and governments – but it proves counter-productive in the longer term. It fails those who most rely on the principles behind our welfare system.

It is time for a new social settlement. At its heart must be a compelling vision for why we require a welfare system and its unique position in national life. We should establish clearly how it can serve those who need it and those who fund it. The moral basis for our welfare system – questions of fairness and justice – must be thrashed out.

damaging drift

The welfare system was and remains a wonderful idea. It stands for something truly British – the underdog. At its best, it ensures that this country will never wash its hands of those who fall on hard times. And to those in poverty who crave opportunity, it can represent a hand up and a brighter future. It was founded with the best of intentions and we should be proud of what it represents.

Yet for more than half a century, since the welfare state's inception, governments have reconstituted and refined the system in a piecemeal, incoherent fashion, which has

Index.[12] That is why it is essential that any new welfare settlement not only promotes work at its core but encourages positive, realistic life choices in a broader sense. We have to get behind people's aspirations. We have to cast a welfare system which promotes rather than undermines the things which protect against poverty.

the moral basis for a new social settlement

To acknowledge these defects and seek to re-cast the how and why of welfare doesn't, as some critics argue, constitute an anti-welfare attitude. It is precisely because we hold the purpose of the welfare state in such high regard, because we are so passionate about its meaning, that we should be honest about how it has lost its way. We fail to serve the poor if we turn away from uncomfortable conversations about the safety net we need to improve.

We should be angered by poverty, not poor people. We should be moved that our system has trapped too many people who just need a chance. And, of course, recognition of these failings should be linked to broader economic problems as well as the problems we have unquestionably created ourselves.

Perhaps inevitably, welfare reform has already become a key party political dividing line ahead of the general election in 2015. But in stepping back from the knockabout, there is more consensus than meets the eye. And when considering the moral basis for welfare, there are a number of first principles that politicians and policy-makers could unite behind. The next section will focus principally on working age welfare but older age benefits issues too. Just as Beveridge had his giants, we should develop new founding principles which can serve as the moral basis of a new social settlement.

working age welfare

The dignity of every human being

Everyone matters. When it comes to the most vulnerable and to those who cannot care for themselves, we should be quick to offer unconditional support. The British people should take pride in ensuring that fellow citizens who are ill, old or those who have disabilities which prevent them from working, are never left behind.

Yet we should not automatically lower our ambitions for people with disabilities or other health problems who want a chance to do something. The employment rate for disabled people is 30% lower than it is within the rest of the general population – with sensitive consultation and careful support, this could surely be different.

A nation of the second chance

Through our welfare system we have held back too many people who could become financially independent. We should be unrelentingly ambitious about what people can achieve, and mindful of the consequences when people end up, over longer periods of time, dependent on welfare. The welfare state should be unashamedly focused on helping people realise their full potential at home and in the workplace.

With family stability and work as central objectives, the system could play its part in a wider effort to see the root causes of poverty dismantled. A child in a household where neither adult works has a 64% chance of being in financial poverty. By contrast, a child in a couple household where both adults are in full time work has a 1% chance of being in financial poverty.[13]

The impact of sustainable work can be transformational for individuals, families and entire neighbourhoods. Its ripple effect shows precisely why the welfare state should become a springboard again. The chance of staying out of poverty a year after someone in a family gets a new job is 56%, and this figures increases to 76% when a new full time worker joins the household.[14] Health and wellbeing advantages follow and other social failures are addressed. Humans are by nature industrious and it is immoral to stand in their way. Backing the work choice would also be fairer for taxpayers, who expect people to do what they can to help themselves in return for support.

And as much as we discuss expectations of individuals and claimants, we should be clear about expectations placed on the state. If there is a clear pro-work expectation placed on claimants, there is also a moral obligation for the state to uphold its end of the bargain. To do so, governments need to provide effective back-to-work support that can help people broaden their interests, skills and capabilities. Welfare has lost its second chance mantra. We need to bring it back.

The same choices

People on welfare should, wherever possible, face the same kind of decisions as those who are not on welfare. The system should reflect the same choices that those in work face. It cannot absolve people of their responsibilities because otherwise we make welfare an easier option, we create the conditions for welfare dependency, we make it harder for people to sustain independence from welfare, and we create social resentment.

Key questions here might include whether the state should provide benefits regardless of how many children people have, or whether support should be restricted to a certain number of children? Is the notion of a 'council house for life' an icon of the past and should everyone now face shorter agreements with employment objectives linked to their tenancy? Should we house people in areas they could never afford to live in if they were on the area's average wage? For the 16-year-old leaving school with few or no qualifications, what kind of support would ensure they get help but avoid a life cycling in and out of the welfare system? Should benefits be paid on a monthly basis, as wages are to most people in work?

These policy options are inherently linked with judgements people make about how to live their lives. Much of the hardening of social attitudes towards welfare seems to relate to the fact that people reliant on benefits can have things, in principle, that others cannot.

Focus on need, not redistribution or insurance

There are a number of key questions that confront the welfare system over how much support people should receive and what conditions of entitlement should be attached. With the decline of contributory welfare and the shift to means-testing, the emphasis on assessment of need has become much more pronounced. However, this definition of need now encompasses those high up the income scale. Instead of reducing poverty it has become a mechanism for redistributing income.

The reintroduction of a more contributory system in which everybody receives more is not the panacea some suggest. Although politicians often talk about re-establishing contributory welfare because it plays well amongst certain sections of the British public, spending more money on the welfare budget polls terribly. Therefore, if rewarding contributions through additional welfare payments is off the table because higher spending isn't an option, the primary way to differentiate between those who have paid into the system and those who haven't is to start reducing the level of support that people currently receive in order to give others more. This also leaves open the charge that we identify 'deserving' and 'undeserving' poor, which many also rightly criticise.

Those who argue for the protection and pursuit of the social insurance model – i.e. that because we all pay in we all should get back – miss the point of insurance. Insurance premiums are paid to secure protection if and when it is required, not to guarantee a return regardless of circumstance. Our travel insurance pays out for lost luggage or medical expenses, not safe and uneventful holidays.

Welfare cannot and should not mean something for everybody. That is unaffordable and strange. It should instead focus on those who need help. That way we can make the best use of taxpayers' money and tackle the underlying causes of poverty. At its best in the eyes of the British people, welfare would act as a lifeboat, not a cruise ship.

beyond working age welfare

The welfare state also needs to reappraise its contract with pensioners. Whilst the working age welfare budget has increased substantially, so has the cost of providing support to older people. The working age welfare budget has been reduced by more than £20 billion in the last three years; pensioner benefits such as Winter Fuel Payments have been protected. State pension spending has also risen significantly as a result of the Coalition's triple lock guarantee. Although this needs to be considered in balance with the UK's record low interest rates, which of course work against savers and older people, a deep sense of injustice has built in some quarters.

When many working families are barely treading water and the poorest pensioners have to choose between heating and eating, we should ask whether it is morally justifiable to retain universal handouts for the wealthiest older people. Such politically-motivated universalism sits strangely alongside the main thrust of welfare policy in recent times.

Equally, when the basic state pension was first introduced under David Lloyd George in 1908 it had a qualifying age of 70 years (alongside some other interesting qualifying rules like the requirement 'to be of good character'). Life expectancy, by contrast, was about 50 for men and 54 for women at this time.[15] Now, of course, people in retirement can hope to live for perhaps 20 years beyond the state pension age in good health.[16] A new moral balance needs to be found for retirement and state pension ages – a balance which serves those in retirement and the shrinking working age population that funds it (in 1926 when the state pension age was set at 65 there were nine people of working age for every pensioner. In 2013, there were just three people of working age for every pensioner, and that is set to fall to nearer two by the end of this century).

As a country we should be proud to provide for our older generations in their retirement and to ensure that those who can no longer work are supported. But in view of the impending demographic and economic challenges before us, and in view of some anomalies within the current settlement, sensible reconsideration is due.

seizing the moment

The economic crisis has forced those in office to make difficult decisions about the welfare system. Whatever the rights and wrongs of their actions, this has provided an opportunity for the debate to go back to first principles. These deliberations, by the very nature of the people our welfare system should serve, cannot be amoral.

The welfare system has lost its way and much of its credibility, but that is cause to rescue it, not abandon it. For the sake of those who need it and those who fund it, this is a moment to build an ambitious system which does everything it can to catch those who fall, but then to move them back to work and to stabilise family life when it can. Let it act as a gateway to new skills and interests for those trapped in poverty. And let us design a system for older generations which keeps pace with the ageing society but leaves nobody behind. That would be a moral basis for welfare.

chapter 4 – references

1. HM Treasury, Public Expenditure Statistical Analyses, Table 1.1, Cm8663, July 2013 p. 19.
2. Sir William Beveridge, Social Insurance and Allied Services, Cm6404, London 1942.
3. Institute for Fiscal Studies, "A Survey of the UK Benefit System", November 2012.
4. HoC Library, Social Indicators Page, Social Security Expenditure.
5. DirectGov, "Benefits and help for parents going back to work" link accessed on 08.05.13.
6. http://www.theguardian.com/politics/2013/apr/06/welfare-britain-facts-myths?view=mobile .
7. HM Government, State of the nation report: poverty, worklessness and welfare dependency in the UK, London, HM Government, 2010.
8. Eurostat, "Jobless households – children".
9. ONS, Working and workless households 2011 Table E, 1 September 2011.
10. Liam Byrne, Guardian, 2 January 2012.
11. UC, Impact Assessment, 2012.
12. OECD, Child Wellbeing Index 2011.
13. HM Government, State of the nation report: poverty, worklessness and welfare dependency in the UK, 2010.
14. Written evidence submitted to the CSJ by Joseph Rowntree Foundation.
15. ONS, Projections based on 1911 census.
16. ONS, Historic and Projected Mortality Data (1951 to 2060) from the UK Life Tables, 2010-based.

5

the Church of England and welfare today
Malcolm Brown

In July 2013, the General Synod of the Church of England debated the welfare reforms being introduced by the Department for Work and Pensions (DWP).[1] The impetus for the debate came from the grassroots – from Synod members, clergy and lay, who were meeting more and more people in their parishes whose lives were being affected by the DWP's changes to the system and by the response (or lack of it) from those structures tasked with delivering benefits. Clergy were speaking, in terms rarely heard since the early 1980s, of the vicarage doorstep as the place of last resort for people on the verge of destitution. Contrary to popular perception, the General Synod was not proposing to debate a topic in the abstract but as a way of crystallising a growing disquiet based on experiential evidence gained through the church's presence in the communities most affected by policy changes.

Many have noted that the Church of England has a kind of instinctive love affair with the welfare state. The historical and theological background to that affinity between church and welfare state has rarely been examined and is, I suspect, more of a folk memory in the church – albeit, a folk memory that tends to shape attitudes – than a conscious part of a tradition. This essay considers the roots of that affinity, and examines some of the principles behind a welfare state and the balance between state provision and voluntary action. It draws on other recent and relevant Synod debates to put the welfare changes into a moral context, before concluding with a brief note on the church's response at different levels.

the constantly shifting context

The Church of England is well aware that the changes being introduced by the DWP are driven, in part, by a moral vision and not solely by the prospect of reducing public spending. It acknowledges that two objectives are being pursued: the simplification of a complex system, which embodies numerous perverse incentives and inconsistencies, and the fundamental belief that encouraging people into work is a very proper goal since it is through meaningful work that most people find self-worth and contribute to community life.

Commentators, before and after the Synod, tended to assume that the debate was motivated by a desire to 'kick the government', oblivious to the case for reform. That was simply not the case. Quite apart from anything else, the DWP's moral goals seem to have broad support, in the churches and beyond. That recognised, moral goals can only be pursued through concrete policies, and it was the effect of those policies which was becoming painfully evident to many Synod members.

This was not the first time the Church of England had addressed issues in welfare. It published a major report in 1986 entitled *Not Just for the Poor* (the pun in the title was deliberate).[2] The report remains helpful, not least for presenting issues of welfare as policy dilemmas in which short and long term goals are hard to reconcile. But reading that report now shows how much has changed. For example, what was conceived as a national insurance scheme, largely to offer protection against unforeseen events or misfortunes and intended to build social solidarity, has evolved into a programme to prevent those at the bottom of an increasingly unequal society from falling into destitution. Changing family structures and an ageing population have created new problems and complexities. The link between National Insurance and the benefits due to contributors has largely been broken, although policy makers across the political spectrum are considering how a contributory element might be reintroduced in order to bolster support for the system.

Universal benefits, with the notable exception of pensions, have largely given way to benefits targeted at the most needy. This is regretted by some, on the grounds that it increases bureaucracy and diminishes the commitment of all citizens to the welfare system, but it has probably been inevitable as demands on the welfare structures have multiplied faster than people's willingness to finance them. In all these changes and adjustments through the years, a single, widely supported narrative about the purposes and principles of a welfare system has been muddled or lost.

why the church is right to value a welfare state

If the Church of England really does have an instinctive sympathy for the principles underlying the welfare state, it is worth asking why – and whether such a position is tenable today.

The church has, of course, been deeply involved in the provision of social welfare of various sorts for centuries. The post-war period, when welfare structures were shaped by the famous Beveridge Report of 1942, sets a benchmark against which subsequent changes have often been assessed. Beveridge's thinking was deeply influenced by his lifelong association with Archbishop William Temple[3] who popularised the term 'welfare state'.[4] Temple was seeking to answer a fundamental question: to what kind of state could the Christian give allegiance, given that Christians always bear ultimate allegiance to an authority higher than any state?[5]

Writing when democracy was threatened by totalitarianism, Temple saw clearly that the Christian must reject what Hitler called the Power State, justified by its ability to project the aggression of its leaders. In the light of the Great Depression, however, Temple also rejected the *laissez faire* model. Instead, he concluded, Christians could give provisional allegiance to a state that set out to secure the welfare of its citizens. At a time of war, when many were called to die for their country, the settlement between the state and its people needed to be sufficiently reciprocal. A 'welfare state' might do this in a way acceptable to Christian understandings. Beveridge's report was a practical outworking of this theological position. Christians may continue to hold to the principle that a welfare state can command their allegiance without remaining wedded to every jot and tittle of the Beveridge report, which was a tract for its time, not for all time.

Does that theological position hold today? Christians will always treat the earthly state as provisional, so should they not seek to minimise the role of the state across the board?[6] But even the most minimal state continues to demand a great deal from its citizens. As the Catholic moral philosopher Alasdair MacIntyre has put it, reducing the role of the state to the management of private contracts is "like being asked to die for the telephone company."[7] As long as the state requires its citizens, from time to time, to sacrifice even their lives in its service, people may reasonably ask what the state is prepared to give in return. To ask much from the citizen without any responsibility to secure his or her welfare calls the very legitimacy of the state into question. That is not a justification for particular welfare policies, but it still justifies Christian support for the principle of a welfare state.

the state, voluntary action, and the fate of the big society

Beveridge also wrote a second, less well known report entitled *Voluntary Action*.[8] This reflected his concern that the state should not relieve individuals or communities of all responsibility of care for the vulnerable, the weak or the unfortunate. By the mid-twentieth century, social mobility and individualism had corroded the social bonds that would make local provision adequate on its own; hence the need for the state to provide basic social security to relieve the fear of the 'five great evils' of Want, Disease, Ignorance, Idleness and Squalor. The impersonal state cannot, however, simply replace the structures of civil society and, alongside a welfare state, the regeneration of strong intermediate institutions and structures of voluntary action were essential.

This dilemma has direct relevance to our contemporary political context. Before and immediately after the 2010 general election, much was made in Conservative circles of the Big Society. Those behind this idea sought to regenerate local communities as a way of rolling back the increasingly bureaucratic and impersonal state welfare provision. The Church, at many levels, strongly supported the Big Society principle.[9]

Three years on, we have seen very little of the Big Society. Instead, the voluntary sector is facing a pincer-like squeeze between declining income from giving (normal during a prolonged recession) and considerable cuts to government funding. There is very little to show for the church's strong support for a new settlement between the state and local voluntary action.

The effective abandonment of the Big Society means that the philosophical foundations for a new settlement between the state and voluntarism have been lost. The current round of welfare reforms is seeking to change the relationship between the state and the citizen without the careful rebuilding of local structures that would have offered a real alternative to monolithic state provision.[10]

public perceptions of welfare

The majority of the 'welfare' budget is spent on pensions. Successive governments have found it politically difficult to make serious savings on pensions, although the universal entitlement to certain benefits that go with age, such as bus passes and free TV licences, should perhaps come under renewed scrutiny. The public perception of 'welfare' now focuses on benefits for those out of work, disabled, having large families or generally unable to support themselves above poverty levels.

This has had the misleading and potentially divisive effect on the public debate which has very quickly become one about the 'deserving' and 'undeserving' poor. Unemployment is seen less as a misfortune occasioned by the fluctuating economic cycle and more as a moral matter reflecting a person's willingness to work. Government spokespersons have made political capital out of this, and the distinction between 'strivers' and 'scroungers' has entrenched harsh attitudes towards those whose benefits are being targeted for cuts.

But crude distinctions do not capture the complex reality. A large proportion of benefits and Tax Credits go to working families on low incomes (due to a combination of low pay, underemployment, lack of affordable childcare, and rising housing costs). Around half of all families with children will be entitled to Universal Credit. To its credit, the government is very conscious of this, which is why it is considering introducing ways to encourage low earners to work longer hours and seek higher paid jobs.

fairness, generosity and sustainability

The government faces particular problems in introducing welfare reforms at a time when reducing public expenditure is an overriding objective. When the Synod debated the financial crisis in 2009, there was strong criticism of an economy based on debt, and support for the long-term objective of debt reduction.[11] To argue that the church is wringing its hands about welfare whilst ignoring the moral hazard of debt is simply wrong.

The report for the debate on the financial crisis set out three principles against which economic measures to reduce debt might be judged. They are entirely applicable to the cuts in welfare provision that are part of the government's austerity programme. Synod asked:

- **Is it fair?** Does it give priority to the vulnerable – the young struggling to enter the labour market, and the elderly living on fixed incomes; people in poverty both within Britain and globally?

- **Is it generous?** Does it embody the obligation to give and share our resources with others, especially those less well off?

- **Is it sustainable?** Have the medium and long-term implications been taken fully into account so that the interests of our children's and grandchildren's generations are factored in?

The question of **fairness** is always a problem in welfare economics. There is a tension between seeking simple and transparent systems and the tremendous variations between the circumstances of different people. The more straightforward the system, the less capacity it will have to reflect differing circumstances. But a system that is too complex to negotiate is likely to produce unfair outcomes by default.

Fairness also extends to the ways in which welfare is delivered. For example, the drive to return as many as possible to work has led to some disabled people being deemed fit for work on the basis of a very perfunctory assessment. There is evidence that some local offices have set targets for getting so many people a week off benefits, regardless of the nature of the cases before them. Bureaucratic systems make mistakes – but vulnerable people rely on the system delivering reliably and much hardship can ensue when things go wrong. Underfunding the delivery system can multiply errors.

The notion of **generosity** in welfare provision is always contentious. Indeed, it is a tension within biblical ethics where the community is called (in both Old and New Testaments) to ensure the welfare of the widow, the orphan and the stranger, but where it is also recognised (as St Paul so succinctly put it) that a person who is not prepared to work should not expect to eat. Any system that protects the poor and vulnerable is open to the scandal of the free rider. But the Bible is also clear that this does not justify the neglect of those who require the community's support to survive.

Sustainability in welfare provision turns not simply on economics but on social attitudes. The question of what 'we' can afford depends upon who 'we' are. Global migration has raised new questions about entitlement to the benefits of citizenship. With material inequality so great, the moral case for squeezing welfare recipients is harder to make when the very rich appear to be escaping recession largely unscathed.

The question of welfare dependency cannot be ignored. Whilst the existence of a welfare safety net can encourage people to take creative risks (for instance, leaving a secure job to set up a small business), it can sometimes diminish personal responsibility and detach actions from consequences. Creeping dependency is not sustainable if people are to flourish, although the actual extent of welfare dependency is disputed. The language of human sinfulness may make more sense of this dilemma than the language of policy options. The tension between grace and the persistence of sin is not going to be finally resolved in the fallen world we inhabit.

A society which allows large numbers of its citizens to live in poverty is unlikely to be sustainable. We have seen, since the 1980s, how whole communities hit by economic contraction can sink into a kind of collective depression from which some, especially young men, seek to emerge through violence, gangs and other destructive (and self-destructive) ways of life. The many stories of triumph and endurance in such adversity should not blind us to the fate of far too many people where hope is lost.

a new settlement?

The General Synod called for a 'new settlement' between the state and the voluntary sector on welfare issues. But it would be a mistake to jump too quickly to the idea that the churches could simply pick up the responsibility for, and delivery of, statutory services without the nature of those services being reconceived – otherwise the church or voluntary sector would be no more than the agent of a still over-mighty state. What churches are good at is carefully tailored programmes for addressing tightly defined local needs – the sort of work (such as, for instance, befriending schemes) which are not the kind of thing that can easily be delivered by a bureaucratic, monolithic state committed to a one-size-fits-all approach but which nevertheless reduce the demand on central services (thus generating potential savings) because the local infrastructure of care is richer, more responsive and addresses real need. Where there is no local dimension of this kind, statutory or centralised services can become the only repository for all kinds of needs for which they were rarely designed.

When the church called for a new settlement between the state, the citizen and local voluntary action, it meant this kind of rebalancing – not sloughing off onto volunteers those activities which every community must have and which are the proper responsibility of government. This new settlement seems very far from the current thinking of the DWP. In hard times, people rely on their neighbours as much as on the state. But some welfare reforms, especially in the field of housing benefit, seem almost designed to destabilise people's relationships with their local communities. The 'Bedroom Tax' (officially the 'Spare Room Subsidy') and the cap to Housing Benefit are forcing people to move away from areas where they have roots and informal structures of support. In a more flexible housing market, this might not have been quite so disruptive, but the UK has a housing shortage and the housing stock is ill-designed to offer the flexibility of provision which these welfare reforms assume. Overall, it is not easy to align the current round of welfare reforms with the principles which the Synod debate on the financial crisis offered as a moral guide to economic reform in times of austerity.

the church's response of care

In March 2013, the *Daily Telegraph* carried a letter signed by 43 bishops drawing attention to the stresses and injustices brought about by the government's changes to the welfare system and calling for amendments to the Welfare Benefits Uprating Bill then passing through parliament.[12] Members of the Lords Spiritual contributed strongly to the debates on welfare in the House of Lords, opposed the benefit cap on the grounds that it would have a disproportionate effect on children and proposed reasoned, costed, alternatives which were rejected by the government.

Christian charities are among those drawing attention to the 'destitution, hardship and hunger on a large scale' which has already ensued from the cuts to welfare provision, and pointing to the numbers of people now reliant on foodbanks for sustenance.[13] A Church Urban Fund survey of around 900 churches at the end of 2011 found that more than one in four had a foodbank, ranging from a small cupboard of tinned food to a Trussell Trust foodbank.

The contribution of Christians to hundreds of social action projects which alleviate poverty in many ways is considerable and cannot be adequately enumerated here. It is clear that without action by churches, the plight of many people would be insupportable. This action, part of our witness to the love of Christ and our pursuit of the common good of all, is generously given – but those most involved know that it is not filling the gap left by the cuts to welfare provision.

Other funding cuts are severely hampering the work of numerous charities and volunteer schemes. Programmes of social care are under immense pressure as a result of local authority cuts. The gap between need 'on the ground' and the capacity of voluntary action to respond is considerable – and widening.[14]

Work such as the provision of foodbanks has brought out the best in many churches and local groups. A more balanced settlement between state and civil society is long overdue. But rebuilding a culture of voluntarism, community and local care cannot be made to happen merely by the state's withdrawal from its obligations to the poorest.

the church and government

The Synod and the Church of England as a whole are perfectly well aware that government is difficult, and the problems of welfare are a case study in the dilemmas of governing well. But the church's commitment to a welfare state is not mere nostalgia. It is a theological judgement about what the state should be and should do for its citizens. Where the poor and vulnerable carry a disproportionate share of the burden created by the financial crisis, something is wrong.

The church is not equipped to offer detailed alternative policy options – but there is sometimes (to use an overworked term) a prophetic duty to point out that God's priority for the poor and vulnerable is not being adequately reflected in the life of the nation. The generous willingness of churches to ameliorate the impact of welfare cuts has given them authority to comment publicly. Their work for the common good will continue as long as there is need. But it is far from a whole answer to the problem

chapter 5 – references

1. GS1897. This essay is based on the paper offered to Synod as background to the debate. It was accompanied by two factual papers which detailed the reforms and changes being made to the system and their impact on people in a variety of situations.
2. *Not Just for the Poor: Christian Perspectives on the Welfare State*, Church House Publishing, 1986.
3. See: William Temple, *Christianity and Social Order*, Penguin, 1942,
4. Temple drew on the ideas of Alfred Zimmern and George Schuster, who first used the expression.
5. William Temple, *Citizen & Churchman*, Eyre & Spottiswoode, 1941.
6. See the "Minimal State Theory" of Robert Nozick in his, *Anarchy, State and Utopia*, Blackwell, 1974.
7. Alasdair MacIntyre, "Poetry as Political Philosophy", in *Ethics and Politics*, CUP, 2006, p. 163.
8. William Beveridge, *Voluntary Action: A report on methods of social advance*, G Allen &Unwin, 1948.
9. Synod debated The Big Society in November 2010 – see GS1804.
10. Ministers argue that they have, in fact, done much to move toward the Big Society – they cite the Big Society Bank, the Localism Act and other achievements. These measures have, however, made little real impact on the ability of the voluntary sector to flourish and, perhaps more importantly, there has been almost no discernible transfer of power from central government to local voluntary action. Perhaps the greatest indictment is that the rhetoric of the Big Society has disappeared from political discourse. The most effective politicians know that to achieve a revolution in the relationship between government and the people, it is necessary to change the way people think. The Big Society was conceived as just such a new narrative about the kind of society we are – and in this it has achieved nothing of any substance.
11. GS1719.
12. *Daily Telegraph*, 10 May 2013.
13. *Walking the Breadline*, a report from charities including the Trussell Trust, Oxfam and Church Action on Poverty. May 2013.
14. See, for example, the Church Urban Fund report, '*Holding on by a Shoestring*', on the impact of spending cuts on faith-based voluntary groups in deprived areas.

revisiting Beveridge: principles for affordable, sustainable welfare
Jill Kirby

In creating a welfare state, the post-war generation of British politicians believed they were fulfilling a moral duty, to ensure that all citizens would have access to healthcare, education and a minimum income. But as the cost of the welfare state has grown, to the extent that it now consumes more than half of all government spending, so the British public has become more sceptical about its effectiveness. If welfare is not effective – in lifting the poor, healing the sick and transforming the educational prospects of the most disadvantaged – is it still the best way to fulfil our moral obligations, particularly when the cost is so high?

The founders of the National Health Service believed that its costs would fall over time because it would create a healthier nation. Such optimism now seems preposterous. State pensions represented a modest outlay when male life expectancy was just 66; now it is close to 80 and still rising. From 1948 until 1970, unemployment averaged less than 2%. In such conditions, social security payments could reasonably be described as a safety net, not a way of life. Nowadays, however, there are 3.6 million households in the UK where nobody of working age is in paid employment: that means nearly a fifth of all working age households are entirely dependent on social security.

Opinion surveys suggest that in the last ten years public opinion has switched from supporting generous benefits to believing that social security payments are too high, and are discouraging work. Politicians of all parties are beginning to recognise that their arguments for welfare spending need to change. Rather than boasting of spending more money, they must demonstrate that they are investing wisely, improving social mobility and creating the conditions in which individuals and families can thrive without continual, expensive, state support.

This essay considers the cost of today's welfare state, in particular the social security system, and considers how far it has departed from the objectives of its founders. It reflects on the principles guiding William Beveridge in 1942, as he wrote his best-selling report. Seventy years on, Beveridge's hopes for sustainable, contributory welfare, which would strengthen families and deepen social solidarity, have not been fulfilled. Perhaps if we paid more attention to his guiding principles, we might devise a system that would not only be more affordable but also more sustainable, by increasing scope for contributions and by developing and encouraging personal and family responsibility?

the cost of welfare

Since 2010, the coalition government has embarked on large-scale reforms of the three main components of the welfare state: health, education, and social security payments. Surprisingly, whilst both parties to the coalition maintain that their overriding objective is the reduction of the nation's economic deficit, a glance at public spending figures shows that these reforms have not so far been driven by budgetary constraints. Indeed, the health and schools budgets have both been ring fenced from cuts, the state pension is set to become more generous, and cuts to some welfare payments are likely to be offset by the costs of the new Universal Credit payments.

The Chancellor's recent promise of a government cap on welfare expenditure from 2015 appears to be a belated recognition that the current structural reforms will not bring about savings, so that the only way to limit future costs will be the imposition of an arbitrary maximum. The Labour opposition has already declared its support for such a cap, the only difference from the coalition being that Labour has indicated it would be prepared to limit spending on pensions (the single biggest component of welfare expenditure). So far, however, none of the main political parties seems prepared to discuss the prospect of making real-terms reductions in the cost of welfare provision.

Yet today's welfare state carries a very large price tag. Expenditure on social security payments, including the state pension, currently stands at £220 billion a year. The National Health Service annual budget is £137 billion. That means that half of all today's public expenditure is channelled to health and social protection.

Did the founders of the post-war welfare state ever contemplate the possibility that the cost would soar to such levels? Surely not. Not only would the scale of the figures have been alarming, but the share of government spending would also have seemed extraordinary. In 1948/49 social security payments amounted to less than 10% of spending – now they account for 30% of the Chancellor's annual outlay.

the contributory principle

One of the key reasons why the welfare state is no longer economically sustainable is the fact that payments out are not linked to payments in. Although it was William Beveridge's original intention that the welfare system should be based on the contributory principle, the link between contributions and benefits was broken very early. The Beveridge Report recommended fixed rate payments by both employer and employee into a social insurance fund, which would then pay out benefits to contributors, also at fixed rates. Those benefits would comprise sick pay, medical cover, unemployment, maternity, widows, orphans, old age, and funeral payments. The system was intended to mimic an insurance contract. By pooling risks and resources, the state would act as insurer, but would not discourage self-reliance. Crucially, payments would not be means-tested. As William Beveridge pointed out, means-testing discourages participants from working, or working longer hours.

Yet Beveridge's insurance-based proposals were not followed through. The Attlee government introduced a National Insurance fund, into which mandatory contributions were paid, but it also introduced National Assistance, which paid benefits regardless of contributions. Indeed, the non-contributory, means-tested payments were generally higher than the contributory ones. Combined with the political decision to pay pensions to newly retired people who had not yet made contributions to the Fund, the version of the welfare state enacted in response to the Beveridge Report bore little relationship to several of the key principles laid down by Beveridge himself.

Over the last 60 years, the contributory element of social security has continued to dwindle. In the 1960s, flat-rate national insurance contributions were replaced by earnings-linked, yet higher contributions did not result in higher benefits – these were either flat-rate or means-tested. Gradually, the few remaining elements of social security requiring a contributions record have been reduced or removed altogether.

contributions, morality and affordability

The early substitution of means-testing for the contributory principle immediately removed an important economic constraint. An insurance fund capable of paying out more than it receives cannot be economically sustainable. From the welfare state's inception, therefore, the government has been obliged to make transfers out of general taxation to meet welfare bills. Latterly, as tax receipts have fallen while expenditure continues to grow, the government has been obliged to borrow money in order to pay these bills. Despite the parlous state of government finances, however, there no longer seems an expectation that the country should live within its means, let alone that a welfare system should be self-financing.

Yet, in abandoning the idea of affordability, we have abandoned an important moral principle. One of the reasons William Beveridge believed in a contributory system was that he saw this as the way to ensure social solidarity. A fund into which everyone paid was a legitimate way of sharing risk. Participants recognised that they could end up paying in more than they would ever get out, as with any insurance policy. But the risk-reward trade off was acceptable. In a system where non-contributors are eligible for large payouts, however, resentment soon grows. Hence the modern perception is that the welfare state has become too generous and is no longer 'fair' to taxpayers.

The sense of unfairness is compounded by the realisation that the nation is getting further into debt and that the cost of servicing that debt (some £70 billion a year) is a burden on both present and future taxpayers. Can we continue to incur such liabilities, or should we face up to the problem and work out how to create a genuinely affordable, self-funded system?

The Labour opposition, sensing public anxiety about fairness, has recently raised the possibility that it would restore the contributory principle. In a speech in summer 2013, Labour leader Ed Miliband said "people's faith in the system has been shaken by a system that appears to give a minority of people something for nothing and other people nothing for something." As a step towards dealing with this, he has promised that a Labour government would ensure that those with a longer work record would receive higher unemployment benefits. This may be seen as a first attempt to respond to popular sentiment, but it is also in line with the Beveridge thesis that payments based on contributions improve social cohesion. Some on the left have long argued that the best way to secure the future of the welfare state, and increase its legitimacy, is to uphold the link between welfare and work.

contributory versus means-tested

The main objection to a contribution-based system is the problem which caused the Attlee government to reject it in the first place: what to do about those who have not contributed but are already in need? How do we fulfil our moral obligations to them? There are a number of ways of answering this:

First, by recognising that those who have been unable or unwilling to make a financial contribution have scope to contribute in other ways: through working in social or charitable programmes, or by fulfilling family or caring responsibilities, thereby taking on duties that would otherwise fall to the state or to other members of society.

Second, by doing all in our power to ensure that young people are not drawn into dependency. With the exception of those who are physically or mentally unfit to become independent workers, any school and college leavers unable to find work should not be given benefits but instead offered a paid work programme, enabling them to establish the habit of work and to build up their own record of contributions.

The Coalition government has already introduced a number of such programmes and is increasing the 'conditionality' tests applied to benefit claimants. Acceptance of more stringent work requirements is gradually becoming more widespread, as well as the idea that payments to non-contributors should be constrained. The suggestion that the under-25s, for example, should not receive Housing Benefit, has already been floated by the Welfare Secretary, Iain Duncan Smith. In attempting to restore the 'safety net' principle to welfare, an important first step is limiting its availability, ensuring that social security becomes a last resort rather than a routine expectation.

It is now generally acknowledged that, just as William Beveridge feared, the drawback of guaranteeing income from the state is that adults in receipt of such payments may be less motivated to earn income through work, especially if their wages from employment would be less than, or at best only slightly more than, their income from the welfare system. The proposed new Universal Credit is intended to remove such disincentives to work, by ensuring that everyone will always be better off working than on benefit. Yet it is not the first time attempts have been made to fashion a payment system that always rewards work. Because Universal Credit remains means-tested, recipients who increase their working hours will continue to face high marginal tax rates as credits are withdrawn. Although the rolling together of a raft of different and complex payments into one credit will undoubtedly aid transparency and should reduce some of the disincentives to work, it will remain the case that family breadwinners in particular will have to make difficult choices: do they keep their non-earned income from credits, or do they put in enough extra working hours to lift them clear of dependency? The trap foreseen by Beveridge will still remain.

means-testing and family formation

Another significant welfare trap, which was less predictable in the 1940s but which has been a profoundly damaging side effect of means-tested welfare, is the family trap. In order for families to thrive, welfare interventions should surely be structured to encourage mutual support within families, responding to the natural instinct to help those closest to us. Yet in many cases, welfare policies over the last 60 years have discouraged such interdependence.

As the state has assumed responsibility for financial transfers between families, in its attempt to relieve poverty and smooth out income inequality, so individuals have become less dependent on other members of their own family and more dependent on state provision. Intra-family payments have been replaced by inter-family transfers, mediated by government agencies. Motivated by the wholly admirable desire to ensure no child goes hungry or unclothed, successive governments have developed and enlarged the social security system so that parents are guaranteed a minimum level of income, whether or not they are in paid employment. Family allowances, intended in the 1940s to boost family life and enable parents of young children to live on one income, gradually mutated into a set of payments to mothers. Some of these were universal, such as Child Benefit, others were and are means-tested, such as family and Child Tax Credits, Income Support, childcare payments, and Housing Benefit.

The unintended impact of making payments to mothers, rather than providing allowances for families, has been to reduce interdependency and thus also discourage fathers from taking financial responsibility for their children. If a man's earnings are low or uncertain, his girlfriend may take the view that her income from benefits, including income supplements, is a more reliable way of paying for the cost of raising children than relying on him. For low income couples, the decision to marry or openly cohabit will result in a lower joint income than if they maintain separate households. Changed social norms and the increased financial viability of lone parenthood have combined and interacted to displace fathers. Having ceased to be a financial necessity, fathers have become an optional extra and, in some cases, seen as a liability rather than an active contributor to family life.

In the 1940s, and indeed up until the 1970s, lone parenthood was a rare phenomenon, resulting mostly from bereavement. Now, however, lone parent households now account for 27% of all families with dependent children; only one in ten of these is headed by a lone father. In a quarter of the nation's families, women are raising children alone, and the majority of them are not receiving regular financial assistance from the fathers of their children.

Welfare policies over the last 20 years have sought to encourage lone mothers to take up paid employment and thus become financially independent. But work rates among lone mothers are still much lower than mothers in couples, and more likely to be part-time, supplemented by state assistance. Universal Credit is intended to encourage more single mothers to take paid work, by dispensing with the minimum hours threshold imposed by tax credits. Whilst this will make all forms of part-time work, however modest, more financially viable, it seems unlikely to break the pattern of dependency on income supplements.

Of course, it is reasonable that parents with caring responsibilities should limit their working hours, so as to be able to devote time to raising their children. But because part-time work is unlikely to generate sufficient income to meet all the family's financial needs, the first recourse for support should not be the state but the co-parent.

restoring family responsibility

Couple households share work and caring responsibilities and the income they receive from welfare is assessed on the assumption that they will do so. Where parents live apart, surely welfare payments should also be based on the expectation that they will share work and care? This should not be an impossible task. For example, if all parents were required to attend benefit assessments jointly, whether or not they live together, and have their welfare payments assessed on the basis of joint income, the incentive to live apart (or declare separate households), would be greatly reduced. Such an approach would not only reduce the cost to the state, it would also send an important signal to fathers about their obligations towards their children. It would provide a useful opportunity to demonstrate to both parents that their children need both father and mother to commit to their care and development throughout their upbringing, whether or not those parents are living under the same roof.

As we have seen, a social security system which abandons the contributory principle not only discourages personal responsibility, it also diminishes family obligations. By removing a father's incentives to contribute financially to the upbringing of his children, the state has helped to undermine his place in family life.

conclusion

A welfare state which relies almost entirely on redistributing income from one household to another, and on means-testing households in order to do so, ultimately destroys its own means of survival. If we are to build a sustainable welfare state, we must first recognise and then foster the primary responsibility to provide for our own needs and those of our families.

A good place to start would be to look again at the high ideals espoused by William Beveridge: to remove the work and family traps created by means testing, reinvigorate the contributory principle and create an affordable, self-sustaining, insurance-based system. We cannot claim moral authority for a welfare state which condemns the poor to dependency, breaks up families and continues to pile up debt for future generations.

7

restoring faith in social security
Stephen Timms

a crisis of confidence

The descent from Beveridge has been total. Public attitudes have hardened towards unemployed people, and the political parties now compete to sound tough on 'scroungers'. In setting out their proposals, today's politicians regularly invoke Beveridge, however tenuously, in a forlorn effort to recreate the optimism of that time. But there is no escaping the fact that today's working age welfare system is politically toxic and the public debate about it has become untethered from evidence or a semblance of rational discussion.[1]

This is a good time to be reassessing the moral foundations of social security. Public confidence in the system is low. The government which came to power on a pledge to rebuild confidence is finding that its programmes are – to quote the Chancellor of the Exchequer – "underperforming".[2] Spending on welfare is set to be much higher across this Parliament than was planned in 2010.

Many people think the system is too generous. Others, including people who have contributed throughout their working lives, are dismayed to find that, when they need help, the system actually provides very little. Research commissioned by the Joseph Rowntree Foundation highlights a long term hardening of public attitudes. In 2011, 54% believed that, if benefits were not so generous, people would learn to stand on their own feet, compared with only 33% in 1987. However, the view that the state should be tackling child poverty remains widespread. The same research found that 82% viewed cutting child poverty as "very important", with almost three-quarters (74%) saying it is a task for government.[3]

the welfare state we're in

When the current government took office, it said that its policies would lead to 'steady growth and falling unemployment'. This view has unfortunately proved mistaken. Long-term unemployment has risen substantially, youth unemployment is still close to a million, and unemployment among some ethnic minority groups is at shockingly high levels.

The government's ambitions on welfare have led to a raft of flagship initiatives such as the Work Programme (a unified scheme to help the long-term unemployed), the introduction of Universal Credit (a single benefit designed to reduce the complexity of the welfare system and incentivise work), and the under-occupancy penalty, or 'Bedroom Tax', whereby people in social housing with a spare bedroom have their Housing Benefit cut if they cannot secure a move to an available smaller property.

The Work Programme is a generally sensible development of ideas in previous programmes, but its performance so far has been disappointing. Labour has supported the principle of Universal Credit, but its implementation is proving deeply problematic. The Bedroom Tax is proving particularly harsh. The Papworth Trust has reported its alarm at the number of disabled people cutting back on food or bills as a result.[4]

Increasingly, more and more people have been finding that they can no longer afford sufficient food for themselves and their families. There has been an explosion in demand for charitable foodbanks, most of them church-based and co-ordinated by the Trussell Trust. The Trussell Trust reports that its foodbanks supported 350,000 households last year, a tenfold increase on the number in the year before the general election, and that, at present, one new foodbank is opening every day.

This debate is not new, but the spirit in which it has been conducted has taken on a different character since the financial crisis. It is right that Theos is exploring the ethics of social security. I aim in this contribution to explore the Christian thinking that has shaped development of the welfare state, and how intentional ethical and principle-based approaches might point a way forward.

the faith roots of the welfare state

The debate in Britain about social security is inextricably linked to Christian conceptions of care for the vulnerable and our fellow citizens, the dignity of work and notions of the common good. These are all themes that are central to the biblical narrative. The first labour exchange was set up by the Salvation Army, in Upper Thames Street, London, in 1890. The term 'welfare state' was coined by the Archbishop of Canterbury, William Temple.

The contemporary debate about social security and work (and we should not separate these two notions) requires a deep reflection on the ethical and moral frameworks that should shape public discussion. It is not just faith leaders and institutions that are making the case for this debate. As the journalist David Brindle has written:

> There is a clear feeling that the current debate around our public services is so fundamental that it cannot be left just to politicians and those who run the services. If we are to hack off bits of the welfare state in response to the fiscal crisis, then we face moral and ethical questions that take us back to Temple and those wartime dialectics. Some would say the butchery has already begun.[5]

The Christian faith presents a clear view of the importance of work, support for the weak, and vocation. In the book of Genesis, the creation mandate involves a commission to men and women to work. They are incomplete without it. Work is to be creative and fulfilling – it is part of God's plan. The influential Christian writer John Stott wrote that "work is one of the main ways through which we express what it means to be human".[6]

The commencement of work – especially after a lengthy period without it – can transform a person's circumstances. Work provides income and stability. It is bound up with our identity, and helps us develop character. Lack of work for a long period is dehumanising. Being unemployed means we have been denied a route through which to express ourselves and our humanity. Employment, unemployment and social security are moral and ethical issues.

In addition to this clear sense that God has planned fulfilling work for all of us to do, the biblical vision of society highlights the cries of the needy and the case against injustice. Justice, and concern for fellow humans, are central.

> The Spirit of the Sovereign Lord is on me, because the Lord has anointed me to proclaim good news to the poor. He has sent me to bind up the broken-hearted, to proclaim freedom for the captives and release from darkness for the prisoners.[7]

Concern for our fellow citizens and the poor is inseparable from the work of the church and the mission of Jesus. The 'golden rule' makes clear that Christians cannot just look after themselves and their own kind. "So in everything, do to others what you would have them do to you, for this sums up the Law and the Prophets."[8]

Work is good and God given. Those seeking to follow Him have an explicit social responsibility to others who are less well off. These are sound foundations for an ethical engagement with the question of welfare.

Christians inspired by these convictions about the goodness of work and the basis for social security have always been deeply involved in social action initiatives in these areas. That was the origin of the welfare state in the first place. There is today a new raft of faith-based initiatives which can play an equally important part in a new vision for social security.

a new moral foundation for social security

While most people would accept that religious influences have been key in Britain's history, it is more controversial to argue – as I am doing – that they can also be crucial in the future. Far fewer people attend worship these days, and there is no shortage of observers to assert that faith groups are largely irrelevant in secular, modern Britain.

But I believe that is a mis-reading of what is going on. A recent report by the London Churches Group for Social Action estimated how much social action is being undertaken by faith groups in the London borough of Wandsworth. It concluded that:

> Faith organisations were running 40% of all voluntary sector welfare projects in the borough (35% by Christians and 5% by other faiths). This is at least two or three times the number that might be expected based on, for example, regular church attendance/membership in the borough. An additional 7% of secular projects had been founded by a faith organisation.[9]

If the faith-based contribution to welfare was to cease, the consequences would be dire. As Adam Dinham, Director of the Faiths and Civil Society Unit at Goldsmiths, University of London has observed, "together, faith-based welfare is an essential buttress for state welfare. Without it, the architecture of care would collapse."[10]

In London, participation in faith groups – including the number of people on the electoral role of the Church of England – is on the rise. And, increasingly, faith groups are taking it on themselves to intervene to help their struggling fellow citizens. The rise of foodbanks is a startling recent example. Who else but the churches could have mounted so large and rapid an operation to tackle the emergency? And, if the Archbishop of Canterbury has his way, support from the Church of England for credit unions will see off the high cost payday loan industry.

Church-based initiatives to help people into work are making an increasingly important contribution. The ones I know best are in London. They include organisations like long-established 'Pecan' (Peckham Evangelical Churches Action Network) in south London; 'Spear' based at St Paul's Church in Hammersmith which serves west London; 'City Gateway' which is having a big impact in East London and has been embraced by the *Evening Standard*; and 'Ascend' based at All Saints Church, South Oxhey, north of London.

They are often entirely independent of the government's Work Programme, and can enjoy higher levels of trust as a result.

Valuable initiatives are not confined to those with Christian roots. 'Faith Regen' is a Muslim-led organisation which has shown it can help unemployed people beyond the reach of public sector and corporate agencies. And mosques – plus Bevis Marks synagogue – played an important role in the success of London Citizens in recruiting unemployed Londoners for temporary jobs at the London 2012 Olympic and Paralympic Games.

And the Salvation Army is still on the case. The Salvation Army's 'Employment Plus' team is a sub-contractor on the government's Work Programme. Their report on ways to improve the Work Programme[11] is adorned with a photograph of that first labour exchange from 1890. In Australia, the Salvation Army has long been one of the most important providers of employment support.

The Baptist Union of Great Britain, the Methodist Church, The Church of Scotland and the United Reform Church have been working hard to tackle misconceptions about the welfare system. Their report, *The lies we tell ourselves*, investigates the veracity of claims levelled at the poorest in our society and the functioning of the social security system.[12]

In 1997, the churches' report, *Unemployment and the Future of Work*, set out the broad-based moral argument that, "it is wrong, in so prosperous a society as ours, for large numbers of people to be deprived for long periods of the means of earning a living".[13] That provided an intellectual foundation for the New Deal programme introduced by the Labour Government elected in that year. In the same way, the current profusion of activity among faith-based groups will require a response from the government elected in 2015.

Labour's thinking on social security rests on a set of ethical presuppositions: the refusal to accept long-term unemployment as normative, the primacy of the common good in public policy formulation, and the centrality of reciprocity in social relationships. Labour's policy programme which draws on these ethical tenets contains two key elements: the introduction of job guarantees, and a renewal of the contributory principle.

challenging the scourge of long-term unemployment

We share the view, which characterises many of the faith-based initiatives I have been describing, that people are entitled to the chance to work; and that, once the chance has been provided, unemployed people have the responsibility to take it up. No one should be abandoned to the fate of long-term unemployment. It is deeply damaging to the individuals, their families and society.

The Bible indicates that God is active and has plans for our lives that embody purpose. Work is good, and the absence of work is damaging. God has planned fulfilling work for all of us to do. A biblical vision of society heeds the cries of the needy. Justice and an intentional concern for our fellow man are central to the work of the gospel. This is why unemployment, in addition to being an economic and social concern, is also a theological and ethical concern. God did not create human beings with potential and self-worth merely to be unemployed. Christians are right to be concerned about employment – the availability of meaningful work and the impact of a lack of work on our fellow citizens.

In political terms, this means that unemployment is not a 'price worth paying' for other, abstract economic goals. It is an economic and political failure that dehumanises us. This is why long-term unemployment should not be tolerated as a point of principle. Institutions and policies should be orientated to interrupting the cycle of unemployment.

Labour proposes the introduction of a Job Guarantee. A choice of job offers will be made to every young person who has been out of work for a year, and to everyone aged over 25 who has been unemployed for over two years. The jobs will last for at least six months, be paid at least at the level of the national minimum wage, and be for at least 25 hours per week, with the balance of the participants' working week taken up by supported search for permanent work. Payment of Job Seekers Allowance will cease for six months once the job offers have been made.

The policy builds upon the Future Jobs Fund, which succeeded in reducing youth unemployment in the teeth of the recession. In the Future Jobs Fund, most – though not all – of the job placements offered were in the public or voluntary sector. With our Job Guarantee, particularly for those over 25, we would like as many of the jobs as possible to be in the private sector. The Labour Party has been working on developing this proposal and how it will dovetail with broader policy imperatives such as localised provision and skills policy.

The principle that we don't stand aside and accept a brutal free market approach is shaped by a deep revulsion at unemployment. We should not blithely walk on by as our fellow citizens suffer the confidence-sapping experience of unemployment. There needs to be a strong commitment from those agents (the state, market and civil society) who can shape social and economic structures to break the cycle of unemployment. The Job Guarantee can help embed this principle, and contribute to the flourishing of many.

reciprocity and the centrality of the contributory principle

> In the coming period of austerity, welfare will be a critical political issue. The challenges of labour market volatility, of the soaring cost of pensions and an ageing population, of a tax system in need of redesign, and of restructuring capitalism for wealth creation and jobs, might be better met with a reciprocal, contribution-based system of social insurance which ensures protection and is more politically robust. But it must be one that hard-wires compassion into its structure for those who, through no fault of their own, are unable to contribute. It would involve a massive change, perhaps one that is politically impossible given the welfare traditions in this country. But the present system is failing and the political prize for changing it would be enduring and historical.[14]

In order for modern social security systems to function, the confidence of the working population has to be secured. Thus, the system needs to honour the contributions of individuals who have paid in to it when they look for assistance in hard times. The renewal of interest in the primacy of the contributory principle is allied to the renewal of interest in the principle of 'reciprocity'. That is, social security should function on the basis that an individual gets 'something for something'.

> A re-asserted contributory principle would, it is argued, mean that what people get out of the welfare system is more closely linked to what they put in. This would recognise the importance of reciprocity. A greater focus on reciprocity is also seen as going beyond a simple accounting rule, to express a concern about active relationships of 'give and take' and a rejection of dependence and paternalism.[15]

The principle of reciprocity has deep roots in British culture. There is an ethic of 'give and take', a sense of fair play, the sense that hard work deserves reward. The contributory principle embodies this ethic. If public policy can get nearer to this principle and incentivise virtuous behaviour, then we could see a social security system that commands broader support and the terms of the debate changed. As Maurice Glasman has argued, "fulfilment of your duty to others should be the foundation of the new Welfare Settlement."[16]

There need be no conflict between the reassertion of the contributory principle and the need to protect the poorest. To help the disadvantaged, we need support from hard working taxpayers for the social security system. It should be a political priority to address the root causes of the rising benefit bill and renew the contributory principle in social security. William Beveridge argued that the welfare state has to contain a strong contributory dimension. He wrote that "benefit in return for contributions, rather than free allowances from the State, is what the people of Britain desire."[17]

In his speech at Newham Dockside in June 2013, Ed Miliband said that "the idea that people should get something back for all they've put in is a value deeply felt by the British people."[18] This is the key to renewing public support for social security. That is why Labour's Policy Review will explore how the system can be reformed, recognising that it will have to be done within tight cost constraints. For example, can we reward with extra support people who have worked for longer? Expressing the challenge in financial terms is instructive. According to modelling by the House of Commons Library, somebody who has worked all their life will have paid in £62,000 more (in real terms) than they eventually receive in a State Pension.

By 2015-16, some 280,000 claimants who have had to stop work on health grounds will have lost all the ESA (previously Incapacity Benefit) entitlement which they could previously have relied upon. It doesn't take much imagination to see how aggrieved people feel, when having worked all their lives, they find out that support available to them is so limited. Leaving such significant numbers of people who have contributed to the system with no entitlement undermines confidence in the system. That is why the restoration of the contributory principle and embedding of reciprocity is both ethically coherent and a political necessity.

The welfare state was established by the Attlee government under the influence of the experience of millions of working people in the 1930s and war years. A fresh mandate can only be successful if it reflects the instincts of the people.

the challenge ahead

As faith groups are increasingly recognising, tackling unemployment – and particularly long-term and youth unemployment – must be one of our highest priorities. Government should ensure that people get the chance of work. Having done so, it is entitled to require that those without jobs take up the chances offered.

And social security is a key measure through which we can all contribute to the well-being of one another. We want more people to find that, when they need help, the system recognises the contributions they have made. These are big challenges, but achievable ones. The example and contributions of faith-based groups are helping to prepare the ground.

chapter 7 – references

1. *"Beveridge Rebooted" "From the Magic of Averages to a Crisis of Legitimacy"*, (Ian Mulheirn and Jeff Masters, Social Market Foundation, 2013).
2. *"The Secretary of State for Work and Pensions … will require a difficult drive for efficiency, and a hard-headed assessment of underperforming programmes",* Rt Hon George Osborne MP, Spending Review Statement, House of Commons, 26 June 2013, Hansard Column 314.
3. Public attitudes to poverty and welfare 1983-2011, NatCen Social Research, May 2013.
4. "Disabled people cutting back on food or bills to pay bedroom tax", Papworth Trust, 10 July 2013.
5. "This upheaval of the welfare state demands spiritual intervention", David Brindle, The Guardian, 31 January 2012.
6. *"Issues Facing Christians Today"*, 4th edition, John Stott, Zondervan, 2006.
7. Isaiah 61 v1, New International Version.
8. Matthew 7 v12, New International Version.
9. *"Better off without them?"*, London Churches Group for Social Action, May 2013.
10. "Welfare is sacred", publicspirit.org.uk.
11. The Salvation Army Employment Plus: *"Adding the Plus to the Work Programme"*, July 2013.
12. *"The lies we tell ourselves: ending comfortable myths about poverty"*, - http://www.jointpublicissues.org.uk/wp-content/uploads/2013/02/Truth-And-Lies-Report-smaller.pdf.
13. "Unemployment and the Future of Work", Council of Churches for Britain and Ireland, 1997.
14. p. 7, 'Welfare Reform – the dread of things to come', Soundings, Eds Sally Davison and Jonathan Rutherford.
15. p. 47, "Contributory Welfare – could the concept of contribution-based welfare help re-galvanise support for the system?" Graeme Cooke, Soundings, no 52, Winter 2012.
16. "Analysis – Labour's New Jerusalem", BBC Radio Four, 27 May 2013.
17. William Beveridge, *"Social Insurance and Allied Services"*, 1942, quoted in *"Making a Contribution: Social Security for the Future"*, Kate Bell and Declan Gaffney, TUC Touchstone Pamphlet, May 2012.
18. Ed Miliband, *"A One Nation Plan for Social Security Reform"*, 6 June 2013.

welfare: a Muslim perspective
Shenaz Bunglawala

It seems like an exercise in abstract thinking to consider the moral logic of welfare when our public discourse on the issue is so steeped in consideration of hard realities and harsh perceptions.

The costs of welfare, ever rising, and the regard for public debt render the issue a difficult one to broach from a moral perspective. It seems almost indulgent when what we are fed in a daily diet of news is disdain for the burden of welfare on hard working families and its abuse by 'scroungers', 'immigrants' and the 'feckless' or 'work-shy'. When services are so commodified and welfare presented in largely monetised terms, it is easy to evade a moral bias in our ideas on welfare: who it should serve, why, and can we still afford it? We are so used to thinking of welfare in terms of opportunity cost; the loss of public funds to other essential areas of public spending to ourselves, or the burden of redistributive policies on family budgets, that we often fail to discern the substantial opportunities that welfare offers to those in need or what it says of the kind of society we want to play a part in cultivating.

I have always reflected on the national system of welfare in the UK as embodying the words uttered by the Egyptian thinker and religious reformer, Muhammad Abduh. On his return to his native Egypt after a spell in France he said, "I went to the West and saw Islam, but no Muslims; I got back to the East and saw Muslims, but not Islam." Of course, he said this circa 1886, and no welfare state in sight, but in my travels to Muslim majority countries now it is these words that ring in my ears when I witness the plight of those on the margins of society with no safety net to provide them with security in hard times, nor any effort to exact a modicum of egalitarianism through state-centric wealth redistribution. The contrast with the UK, which in the post-war settlement envisaged a new social contract between citizens and the state, and between fellow citizens, is a stark reminder of the possibility of imagining and institutionalising bonds of citizenship that are real and based on collective moral responsibility.

The issue of tax and redistributive justice cropped up in family discussions this Ramadan when my siblings and I were all faced with our annual Zakat levy, the 2% wealth tax that we must pay during the holy month to purify wealth and shoulder our responsibilities to those less fortunate than ourselves. For the first time in all the years we've been paying our dues, my brother asked if we were compelled to pay a separate tax on wealth when our incomes are taxed at source and used to pay for welfare at home and abroad, in the form of international aid? I will come back to this later, but here I want to explore further my ruminations on the issue of welfare and redistributive justice from a Muslim perspective.

There are numerous verses of the Qur'an that relay the significance of charity and obligations to the destitute, hungry and needy in society as forms of worship. There are Prophetic sayings which stress the centrality of collective responsibility to one's piety; the one is predicate on the other. Faith is not just about the practice of ritual, personal and regular, but participation in collective endeavours and individual sacrifice for social solidarity. Muslims are urged to care for those less fortunate, those in want, the elderly, and the young.

The two most related *ahadith* that capture this mutuality are the attributed sayings of the Prophet Muhammed:

> He who sleeps on a full stomach whilst his neighbour goes hungry is not one of us (Bukhari)

> He is not of us who does not have mercy on young children, nor honour the elderly (Tirmidhi)

The welfare state, through its system of entitlements and benefits, to me encapsulates the moral injunction to shoulder responsibility for the poor and hungry, the young and the old that Islam commands. The willingness of citizens to participate in this state-managed process of wealth redistribution is, in my view, evidence of the moral ties that bind us together. The popularity of the post-war settlement and the political consensus it enjoyed and still enjoys, though measured and constrained by changed economic fortunes, evinces the rootedness of the idea of collective responsibility. What do we do then when 'willingness' is contested and a dominant morality finds itself challenged by a value pluralism that has no single moral code as its source?

If the idea of the post-war settlement was to foster a new contract between fellow citizens, how citizens relate to one another in an age of mass communication, open borders (at least within the EU) and ethnic, linguistic and religious diversity is a pertinent question. David Goodhart, in his cover essay in *Prospect* magazine in 2004, 'Too Diverse?', tackles this very question and proposes a number of policy interventions to mitigate the risk of diversity undermining solidarity.

The emphasis therein on revitalising teaching on British history and asserting a coherent national narrative about who 'we' are, and how 'we' got here, is certainly evident in the educational reforms introduced to teaching in the school history curriculum. Evident too is the onus on English language competency and the celebration of citizenship through ceremonies. But does the effacing of a fractious diversity through pronounced solidarity make it easier for us to relate to one another? Are the bonds of citizenship more keenly felt, both abstractly and in reality, through a sense of shared commitment to welfare provision and its entitlement, and do we confidently perceive fellow citizens are 'one of us' as a result? I'm not so sure.

Take the example of British Muslims. I have read and studied empirical evidence that demonstrates the affinity British Muslims evince for national institutions, for parliamentary democracy, and the value or primacy they attach to their British identity. Gallup, the Open Society Institute, Demos, and the Centre on Dynamics of Ethnicity at Manchester University are just some examples of survey data that has been captured and analysed in the years since 9/11 and the London bombings of 2005.[1] I witness it too in my work with Muslim civil society. And the perception and reality are poles apart.

Muslims are routinely represented as welfare dependents quite unlike other migrant communities who have shown their commitment to the Protestant work ethic and Britain's entrepreneurial spirit by getting on in life and off welfare. The purported abuse by Muslims of the welfare system has animated far right social movements into reactionary revolt against what they consider appeasement by the political classes.[2]

Consider the findings of the British Social Attitudes survey of 2011 on migration and particularly migration from Muslim majority countries. The BSA survey reveals a majority in favour of reducing immigration. It also records negative sentiments in relation to the economic and cultural impact of immigration. Consistent with what has been documented elsewhere, on the shift in focus on media representations of Islam and Muslims from violence to culture and value compatibility, the 2011 BSA shows an increase in the number of people who view the cultural impact of immigration as 'very bad' from 9% in 2002 to 21% in 2011. Attitudes towards Muslim migrants in the survey is somewhat mixed, with Muslim professionals faring well but with Muslim students facing higher negative sentiments than students from eastern European countries.[3] The survey maps well onto the way the immigration debate has played out in the British media: professionals are wanted, students, with their abuse of the visa system and unwelcome overstays, are not.

The survey also offers insight into the racialisation of 'welfare abusers': Asian students, Muslims in polygamous marriages and those supported by our welfare system through a 'jihad seekers allowance' while they agitate and incite violence against 'us'.[4] These are some of the stereotypes that prevail in the British media about Muslims. Little surprise, then, that the BSA findings should reflect sterner views on Muslim migrants arriving to our shores than other minority groups.

It won't do to hit back with counter-stereotypes of the white working class single mother with a large brood, or errant father hunted down for child support payments to multiple families. Tit-for-tat rivalry and the use of either constituency as a political football to arouse indignation amid calls for welfare (and immigration) reform draws us back to the moral logic of welfare.

The moral logic can't be divorced from the compass that sets its orientation. The logic of welfare and its moral bias is part of something deeper, more embedded in our relational dynamic with others. Are those who look like 'us' the ones deserving of our support? Are those who subscribe to the linguistic and cultural traits of our nation more likely to invite our empathy? As a Muslim, I would say, no. The moral logic of welfare cannot and should not, in my view, be reduced to a civic form of solidarity such that we determine the validity of claims to welfare by the extent to which claimants are more, and not less, like 'us'. It makes me uncomfortable to preface considerations on the size and distribution of the welfare state with a discriminating regard for the end-user. It also seems disingenuous to me to undertake a cost-benefit analysis to assess whether someone drawing out of the common pool has contributed a requisite sum to it. And it is surely unfair to project this onto the worst afflicted in our society while we witness huge disparities of wealth made possible through tax avoidance?

It does not seem to me to be a luxury to probe the moral logic of welfare even if the basis for necessary reforms is driven by imperatives of reduced budgets and growing demands. Our responses to many aspects of welfare provision is instinctively moral: from the indignation at care home abuse of the elderly, to the faith and voluntary sector's rising number of foodbanks to keep families from hunger. It is the moral logic that underpins welfare that serves as a reminder that empathy is not to be conditioned by familiarity but by a consciousness that transcends the narrowness of limited horizons.

Perhaps the strong sentiments expressed in this debate are to be expected as mainstream parties clamour to dispel the traction that xenophobic views have gained in recent years, fuelled by a steady dripfeed of stories on welfare free-riding and class-based hostilities over entitlement. Popular opinion on welfare is easily guided by such repetitive and relentless representations of welfare abuse but it only reinforces the importance of public education on migrant contributions to the economy and political leadership comfortable and confident with diversity and value pluralism. If recent statements on 'health tourism' are anything to go by, both are failing drastically.[5]

To return to the dilemma of paying *zakat* alongside income tax, I would (did) happily pay both in the knowledge that neither money nor welfare is the ultimate object. The objective is personal sacrifice for social solidarity and ritual purity. In short, this is about more than money.

By keeping the question of moral good in the foreground of our collective deliberations on how the post-war settlement must be recalibrated adequately to respond to straitened economic times, I am hopeful that we may yet successfully repeat the exercise and "embody the whole spirit of the Christian ethic in an Act of Parliament".[6]

chapter 8 – references

1. The Gallup Coexist Index 2009: A Global Study of Interfaith Relations (Gallup Inc., 2009) ; Muslims in Europe: A Report on 11 EU Cities (Open Society Institute, 2010); Max Wind-Cowie and Tom Gregory, (2011). '*A Place for Pride*' (Demos) and Stephen Jivraj, 2013. 'Who feels British? The relationship between ethnicity, religion and national identity in England,' The *Dynamics of Diversity: Evidence from the 2011 Census*. (Centre on Dynamics of Ethnicity (CoDE), University of Manchester).

2. Abdulkader Sinno, Eren Tatari, Scott Williamson, Antje Schwennicke and Hicham Bou Nassif, 'Discourses on Muslims and Welfare across the Atlantic,' in *An American Dilemma? Race, Ethnicity and the Welfare State in US and Europe*. Sonya Michel, Klaus Pedersen and Pauli Kettunen, eds. (Washington, D.C.: Woodrow Wilson Center Press, forthcoming, 2013).

3. Park, A., Clery, E., Curtice, J., Phillips, M. and Utting, D. (eds.) (2012), *British Social Attitudes: the 29th Report*, (London: NatCen Social Research).

4. 'Claim Jihad Seeker's Allowance', *The Sun*, 17 February 2013.

5. 'Health tourism: government propaganda that disguises the facts', *The Observer*, 27 October 2013.

6. Archbishop William Temple's description of Beveridge's report.

contract welfare: back to basics
Frank Field

This chapter examines three recent political eras of welfare in this country. It begins with the drive by Beatrice and Sidney Webb to establish a national minimum. This section I have entitled *The Webbs and the Quest for the Minimum*. The chapter then looks briefly at the attempt by the state to raise the stakes by redefining this minimum at a level achieved by some of the best industrial welfare schemes. This section I've called *From the Webbs to Barbara Castle*.

This noble effort failed, and was seen to be failing long before the current bank-led economic crisis. The third theme is therefore a reassessment in current circumstances of the Webbian ideal of a national minimum and how this might operate in an age of trying to bring the national accounts into some form of balance. This section I have headed *Forward from the Webbs*.

First then, let me bring the Webbs back into our discussion.

the Webbs and the quest for a minimum

There has been no more extraordinary couple in Labour party politics than Sidney and Beatrice Webb. And there have been fewer people whose thinking and strategy have exerted influenced across parties than this amazing two-person pressure group.

As well as writing an 11-volume history of local government and the poor law, they produced what became the standard history of British trade unions. Through their research, the Webbs were hoping to discover, as were so many other observers at the time, not simply the social laws that govern society but, more particularly, the mechanisms that might account for the great social and economic advances that so characterised the period through which they were living.

Their volume on trade unions suggested that the skilled trade unions' industrial strength was such that they could win for their members a share in the country's rising prosperity and that, quite simply, this group's collective bargaining power stemmed from the fact that it controlled access to their craft. It had, in other words, the power to hold employers to ransom. What then of the masses of unskilled workers whose sheer numbers invariably guaranteed their surplus in the labour market and for whom, therefore, effective collective bargaining appeared as only a distant possibility? The role played by industrial muscle in securing such gains for skilled trade unionists, the Webbs concluded, had to be secured by parliament legislating a minimum that applied universally so as to cover the semi-skilled and unskilled alike.

Here, then, was the strategy that influenced not just Liberal government insurance-based welfare in the early years of the twentieth century, but Beveridge's proposals which culminated in his famous wartime revolutionary blueprint, and the follow-through actions of the 1945 Labour government.

The first insurance measure under the 1906 Liberal government did not attempt to produce a minimum income in the sense that we think of it today as one lifting people free of poverty. Policy makers then did not think in those terms. A very different model of social advance occupied their minds. For them the question was of building a floor which itself would encourage people to build on by their own efforts. Reformers were anxious not to neuter the drive for good that self-interest could produce. So the first of the modern welfare state insurance measures compelled insurance cover against life's regularly inflicted tribulations of unemployment and sickness. The inability to work through old age had already been covered by what was known as the 'Mr Lloyd George' – the name given by many grateful recipients of Lloyd George's five shilling a week old age pension. All three measures provided a mechanism by which a defence could be built to prevent the respectable poor falling into the clutches of the poor law. Claimants were expected to add to this base by one or more of the insurance policies that were offered by trade unions, mutual or friendly societies, or from the industrial insurance companies like the Pru.

It didn't, of course, work out quite as simply as this, particularly once unemployment insurance cover had been extended to workers outside the tightly defined groups covered by the first Act. The failure to gain an adequate cover from supplementary sources of income led Beveridge to argue that his insurance minimum alone should be adequate in preventing claimants from becoming poor providing they qualified for the full insurance benefit.

from the Webbs to Barbara Castle

There is a considerable literature that believes it answers the question 'why Beveridge failed' when the 'failure' had little to do with Beveridge and much with the actions or, more importantly, the inactions and lack of responsiveness of politicians who failed to notice the major changes that were engulfing their country. If the Beveridge scheme had been viewed more as the living organism, not treated as though Mr Attlee had brought down the Mount Sinai welfare tablets of stone, the outcome might have been very different. Beveridge's insurance approach could have been adapted to the range of social and economic changes that have characterised Britain, particularly since the middle of the post-war years.

Instead of seeing welfare as a living organism, this crucial debate was overshadowed by the ideological battle that was being fought within the Labour Party over what Socialism was about. Labour historically saw a socialist commonwealth as being realised by the common ownership of the means of production, distribution and exchange. This vision increasingly came under attack by a group that went under the name of the Revisionists. The Revisionists, who for a time won the argument, saw Labour's goal as being one about equality, although there was far from unanimity, even amongst themselves, on what in practice was meant by this term.

The Revisionists were, however, successful enough to shift the welfare debate away from seeing the need to establish an adequate minimum to one where a more generous system of wage and salary-related insurance cover was offered, even though all the published data were beginning to show that this minimum ideal was becoming an ever more remote goal. The movement to wage-related benefits marked a fundamental change in the objectives of welfare. The new goal was about securing greater equality of income over each person's lifetime. This took preference now over the original welfare goal of combating the income gaps between classes. While these earnings-related supplements, as they were called, to sickness and unemployment pay were part of this package, the biggest and most expensive innovation came in the introduction of superannuation, the regular deduction from employees' incomes towards a pension scheme. A new age had dawned, or so it seemed.

What is most surprising about the lurch to earnings-related benefits was how little discussion there was of just how fundamental this change was to the welfare state. The ground had been prepared by the Tories in 1959 when the social security minister, John Boyd Carpenter, introduced the most modest of earnings-related additions to the state pension. But this new era began in earnest in 1966 with earnings-related supplements to unemployment and sick pay. Yet these measures were advocated not on the grounds of greater equality – it is ironic how little the social security debate was then influenced by the idea of equality – but on the grounds of promoting the labour flexibility that was demanded by the National Plan the 1964 Labour Government devised and adopted.

The National Plan was the most ambitious British experiment ever in voluntary planning by signing up to achieve national targets. It failed in its noble objective to raise the long-term growth rate of the British economy. Its failure, however, marked in fact, another defeat for a distinct Labour Party ideology where neither nationalisation nor planning could be easily seen as a sure road to socialism. Both propositions were now viewed by voters as being bankrupt.

The 1964-1970 Labour government had attempted to implement Richard Crossman's grand scheme of national superannuation which initially failed as it was not introduced until late in the parliament. The measure, however, was resurrected by Barbara Castle during the 1974-1979 government, and introduced this time early on in the new parliament. Barbara Castle's national superannuation proposals were without doubt by far and away the most significant change in the nature of post-war welfare. Yet, although the most significant alteration to Beveridge's ideal, they were passed without any discussion of why the principle of earnings-related benefit should be adopted.

Mrs Castle's defence of the scheme was that when Beveridge produced his 'great national insurance scheme' everyone believed his proposals would end poverty and deprivation in old age. But that objective, Mrs Castle proclaimed, had not been realised, asserting that "there was now widespread recognition that his aim cannot be achieved by a system of flat-rate contributions and flat-rate benefits." That assertion was at best only half true. For, with irony heaped upon irony, the initial stages of Mrs Castle's bill took off the statute book the Tory pension proposals that paid out [largely] flat rate benefits paid for by income-related contributions.

Labour's superannuation proposals had hardly had any time to bed down before Mrs Thatcher's second government pared back the costs of what many saw as this brave new welfare. The cost of superannuation had come in at £200m in additional payments by 1986 but was scheduled to reach £25.5bn by 2030 measured in 1986 prices. The cost of running the flat rate and earnings-related pensions that then stood at £16bn, would rise three-fold to £49bn by 2033, even if these increases were indexed to prices and not to the more generous index of wages. With only a decade on the statute book, the financial knife was taken to what had become known as SERPs. The government was running scared. Costs did for earnings-related welfare. And in its demise, there was little discussion of the fact that wage-related benefits entailed costs that voters were not prepared to meet, let alone of where this failure led in terms of the purposes of welfare, or of the fact we had embarked upon this brave new world even though millions of our citizens were struggling to keep their heads above the poverty line.

So, where next? And, in particular, where next in an age of austerity?

forward from the Webbs

The current budget deficit is new only in its size. In the first 64 years since 1948, 50 years have recorded budget deficits. Political parties have consistently promised more than they know they can raise in revenue to cover their programme's costs. This unspoken fiscal pact between political parties and voters is now such an ingrained part of our political culture that it will be difficult, not simply in the short run, but probably more importantly in the longer run, to eliminate and then keep the budget in balance.

Not only in most post-war years has there been a budget deficit, but the size of our GDP spent by the government has risen – remarkably so. Within this rising budget, welfare, health and education have taken not only the lion's share, but have outstripped the growth of all other parts of the government programme. Since the war, welfare has always been the largest single government expenditure and its growth has been at a faster rate than other programmes.

Welfare's budget, as part of the new politics of balancing the budget, is being hit, and is likely to continue to take a bigger hit than other parts of the welfare state. It is easy prey; much of it is now the least liked part of welfare state expenditure and this dislike centres on means-tested welfare that grew like Topsy under Magaret Thatcher and Gordon Brown.

There is, as a consequence, widespread voter support for this policy of retrenchment. Yet, in truth, we are in an age when welfare expenditure needs to increase. Our population is ageing and the growth in the proportion of the elderly population will push up the pensions bill as a proportion of GDP. Likewise, as people live longer, they will make increasing demands for health and care services. The Institute for Fiscal Studies estimates that without structural changes to current trends, health and state pensions alone will take 50% of the total government expenditure by 2060. This scenario will not occur, of course, because of the sheer strength of the political backlash it will produce. But for this scenario not to occur will involve some very painful adjustments, particularly for politicians.

Politicians will either have to take on the pensioner lobby, who have a track record of being the most effective group amongst the electorate in getting their own way, or they can attempt to establish a new tax/benefit contract. I much favour this latter strategy. How might this be achieved is staring us in the face. It is, in fact, to reassert the primacy of insurance-based welfare. That is what the taxpayers want. It is politicians who have wilfully refused to do what the voters wish in reforming welfare.

To help an insurance-based contract that is struggling to be born, two moves are paramount. The first is publicly to admit that a welfare strategy that merely reflects and reinforces society's inequality, by giving more to those who already have most, has failed.

There is, secondly, the need to commit ourselves to a Webbian approach of achieving that universal minimum or, as it might be put, to adopt a Heineken-like welfare state. We have never established a minimum income floor in a manner which is approved by taxpayers. These hard to reach parts of society were largely ignored by the earnings-related venture. A renewal of a national minimum attempts to reverse this failure with its new conditional, contract-based welfare model.

A number of advantages would flow from this admission and commitment. Achieving a minimum that has never before been universally achieved would have its appeal. But, as we will see, much will also flow from effectively enforcing an insurance minimum. We will realign welfare so that it works with, rather than against, human nature.

So how might taxpayers be persuaded to enter what will be a new welfare/tax contract?

Taxpayers are unlikely to contribute more of their income in tax under the current rules of engagement between government and themselves, i.e., the government spends revenue as it thinks best with increased resources from taxpayers being spent on means-tested assistance. That has been the record since Mrs Thatcher's welfare revolution.

A growing proportion of the electorate sees means-testing as unfair, yet it is this self same group that is called upon to meet most of welfare's growing bill. It is also this self same group of taxpayers that see means-testing rewarding behaviours and attitudes with which they disagree, often strongly. There is growing voter resistance, therefore, on two fronts – to increases in taxation and then, as if by adding insult to injury, to commanding this hard-earned income and spending it on those parts of welfare that reward those characteristics of which taxpayers most strongly disapprove.

Here, then, is the basis for the transformation that could occur in our society where taxpayers will square up to the growing demand for welfare in an age of austerity, but only if they are allowed their way by politicians conceding a welfare counter-revolution.

That counter-revolution can be easily stated. From early on in the post-war years, a silent welfare revolution was set in hand which became transformative during the Thatcher years and was followed by Gordon Brown's tax credit strategy. Welfare that was provided on the basis of contribution, i.e. on an insurance record, was increasingly replaced by welfare that simply delivered on the basis of need, i.e. recipients could prove their low income. Voters were never given a say in this revolution, although they had to pay for it.

The welfare reform counter-revolution that awaits a radical government is, therefore, to give effect to the twofold wishes of contributors. First, voters disapprove of welfare being given primarily on the basis of need, i.e. my income is below a certain level so I have a right to benefit. Means-tested welfare must therefore be capped and then reduced.

This can be achieved by implementing a second wish of taxpayers. They aspire to see a steady growth in an insurance-based welfare where entitlement is clearly and strictly linked to the monies paid into the scheme, or is gained by a function claimants carry out, i.e., tasks such as caring for increasingly frail relatives, for here are activities voters strongly support. Moreover, the independence of these schemes needs to be secured. I propose that national mutuals be established with independent trustees that should run the new insurance-based welfare state.

Contract welfare, like means-tested welfare, is rich in values. But instead of teaching that it doesn't pay to work, to save and be honest, as does means-testing, contract welfare teaches the opposite values. By guaranteeing a minimum which is claimed on the basis of past contribution, and not on current income, people are encouraged to save, as their savings will not disqualify them from benefit. It likewise encourages honesty. There is no penalty in being honest in having savings, or for one's partner to work, for it makes no difference to one's benefit entitlement. Both potential sources of income are totally disregarded in the eligibility for insurance-based benefit.

It was such a world where these virtues were practised to the public good that Mr Attlee saw as the central part of the good life he was attempting to establish. It is time we again became invigorated by that vision. It will serve Britain's economic needs. It will likewise reward similar social benefits to society. Above all, it will raise hopes of the decent majority that, at last, politicians are not merely listening, but acting in accordance with those taxpayers' wishes.

post-liberal politics and the alternative of mutualising social security
John Milbank and Adrian Pabst

introduction

State welfare is commonly seen as opposed to market capitalism. The right has tended to view it as an arbitrary restriction on free competition, whereas the left has typically associated it with necessary intervention in the workings of a capitalist economy. Either way, both fail to acknowledge that the welfare state, since its emergence in the late 19th century, has not so much transformed capitalism as compensated for some its worst effects (including mass unemployment, poverty and social exclusion) without resolving the underlying conflict between capital and labour. Paradoxically, state welfare has eventually led to the extension of the market into hitherto autonomous areas such as health, employment or education. These had once been more mutually managed by voluntary associations, typically organised by the churches or self-organised by the workers.

To begin with, the British welfare state was understood as a mutual insurance compact against the worst natural and social threats to human survival and flourishing. But in time it has come to be dominated by its other genealogical root, which is the originally Prussian desire for more efficient and quasi-military management of civilian populations.[1] From this perspective, the 1945 and the 1979 welfare settlements represent two sides of the same coin: the former shifted the emphasis towards nationalisation while the latter accentuated privatisation – but both promoted impersonal universalisation and predictability. In different ways, both relied on the strong state and centralised power at the expense of intermediary institutions and popular participation. Crucially, both further fragmented mutual organisation and undermined the pursuit of reciprocal benefit based on contribution and reward. Together they have produced our present reality, which is continually controlled by impossibly distant external forces rather than created through our own efforts, individual and communal.

Linked to this is the twin triumph of social-cultural and economic-political liberalism, which underpins the continual convergence of state and market. Blair's and Cameron's centrism embodies the consensus of the liberal left and the liberal right that disembeds the economy from society and re-embeds social relations in a transactional, economistic and utilitarian culture. As Anthony Giddens put it in his book *The Third Way*, the aim of rationalised 'market-state' welfare is to produce freely-choosing, reflexive and risking individuals who are removed from the relational constraints of family, locality and tradition.[2] In this manner, welfare has become centralised, disjointed and impersonal.

The failure of the 1945 and 1979 settlements is now plain for everyone to see: neither remote bureaucratic control nor internal competition has worked; when combined they have delivered disaster. In the wake of such manifest failure, there is an even greater case for mutualising social security. This is not just about linking rights to responsibilities (as every politician since Thatcher has advocated) but also about solidarity (mutual assistance based on personal need) and subsidiarity (decision-making at the most appropriate level that upholds the dignity of the person and promotes human well-being). In these ways, mutualising welfare involves greater economic justice and a renewed emphasis on interpersonal relationships, supportive of loyalty and belonging to the family, community and locality without wanting to decree the nature of these social bonds. Such paradoxical combinations are characteristic of the new 'post-liberal' politics, for which 'Red Tory' and 'Blue Labour' have been crucial catalysts.

The post-liberalism to which we adhere in this essay seeks to fuse greater economic justice with social reciprocity by promoting both individual virtue and public honour. It rejects the double liberal impersonalism of commercial contract between strangers, and individual entitlement in relation to the bureaucratic machine. Instead of the mixture of contract without gift, plus the unilateral and poisoned gift from nowhere that is state welfare at its worst, it proposes gift-exchange or social reciprocity as the ultimate principle to govern *both* the economic and the political realm.[3] This would transform politics and the economy away from abstract standards and values associated with the prevailing technocratic managerialism towards the dignity of the person and human flourishing within a common polity based on a shared *ethos* of work, saving, caring and honesty.

from means-testing to insurance-based welfare

The welfare system is a veritable state within the state. Since the Attlee government put in place the post-war settlement, real government expenditure has gone up over four times and social security nearly fifteen-fold. As Frank Field MP has remarked, "the biggest growth has been since 1979 with Margaret Thatcher and Gordon Brown revolutionising welfare into a something for nothing contract, amazingly for two puritans."[4] It may further amaze that Thatcher as a disciple of Hayek should have proved an equally adept disciple of Bismarck, but this apparent paradox is revealed as coherent through the post-liberal critique. Where reciprocity is denied in the market in favour of the contractual coincidence of individual self-interest, it is also denied to welfare, reduced to a 'social security' issue of providing a minimum for society's losers.

This sort of reduced welfarism props up free market capitalism, especially the low-wage, low-productivity, low-innovation, and low-growth model that has characterised Britain for much of the post-war period and is now undergoing a 'zero-hours' intensification. The social security budget has grown exponentially over time because welfare has operated as a substitute for high employment, decent jobs with proper pay and widespread asset ownership. (Here the excessive concentration on housing as the one universal asset has proved as much a burden and a bind for people as it has proved a real source of independence, initiative and economic expansion.) Thus, taxpayer-funded welfare is subsidising corporate profit and bloated bureaucracy, each characterised by excessive top-level pay and poor productive performance. They are part of a larger self-serving elite (including many in politics) who brand the workless as 'shirkers' and 'skivers' but fail to honour the mutual obligation which they demand of others.

So it is because responsible reciprocity does not feature enough in mainstream thinking that the direction of travel has been misguided. Nor is it being genuinely redirected, even if Ed Miliband and especially Jon Cruddas have of late outlined a more mutualist vision, including tackling low pay, rewarding work, recognising contribution and a radical devolution of social security policy to local councils.[5]

Consider the coalition government's wide-ranging reform of the benefits system. This, in summary, involves three things. First, switching from a confusing number of myriad entitlements to one Universal Credit. Second, ensuring that those who pass from unemployment to work do not lose too much benefit all at once, while breaking dependency and increasing the motivation to take up employment through guarantees that it will 'pay to work'. Third, an extended programme of 'workfare' with somewhat increased sanctions against those who refuse to take jobs or won't do voluntary work in the community.

The first two components can be seen as belonging to the 'Big Society' aspect of the government agenda, which the Work and Pensions Secretary Iain Duncan Smith has taken forward (frequently in defiance of the Treasury diktat). They may result in a net transfer of resources from the relatively well off to the poor. However, the Universal Credit system (the coalition's flagship reform) merely reduces the marginal tax rate at which recipients decide whether to work longer or train for a better paid job from what was 90% to 65% – still 20% more than the top tax rate. Thus, there is still a considerable disincentive to take up employment, especially for shorter working hours compared with full time employment – a trend of this 'recovery' that is exacerbated by zero-hour contracts. As the House of Commons Work and Pensions Committee has established, the single benefit will cause some of the most vulnerable members of society additional hardship (e.g. monthly instead of weekly payment made to one person per household; a complex online system inaccessible to people without IT skills, etc.).[6] This charge also applies to the 'Bedroom Tax' and other recently introduced changes.

Moreover, the Universal Credit system reinforces the isolation of benefit recipients and the humiliation of face-to-face assessments with contracted healthcare professionals who are unknown and alien to claimants. The continuous reliance on means testing perpetuates the passive dependency and disincentives to work that the reform purports to reverse. To quote Frank Field again: "Well over 22 million citizens already depend on means-tested assistance. Means tests paralyse self-help, discourage self-improvement and tax honesty. Means tests attack the basis of independent citizenship and community cohesion and at the same time incentivise bad behaviour."[7] Crucially, means testing undermines individual virtue and responsibility, alongside public honour and realistic generosity.

However, the fiscal constraints in the next parliament and beyond make universal payments such as Child Benefit unsustainable, as they reinforce the trend of subsidising the affluent and the rich while the poor and the 'squeezed middle' struggle to make ends meet. The alternative to either draconian cuts plus means testing or a ballooning welfare budget is a two-fold contributory model: first, an expanded version of the current National Insurance system to insure everyone against risks like unemployment or the inability to work; second, funding the NHS by creating a new insurance system (modelled on health care mutuals in Scandinavia, Germany and France) – with a contribution from general taxation (much lower than the current health budget) to cover those who cannot pay for health insurance.

To avoid central government meddling and a permanent managerialist revolution, the NHS should be run as a mutual trust accountable to its members (especially patients and front-line staff), with a much greater role for healthcare cooperatives that are co-owned by citizens (not just partnerships among qualified professionals).[8] Linked to this is the case for incorporating social care into the NHS to integrate all of peoples' needs (physical, mental and social) and tailor treatment to the whole person. Just as the NHS should include social care for the elderly, so mutualised welfare should shift the focus away from dealing with the effects of problems (e.g. unemployment, ill health, etc.) towards tackling the root causes through early intervention.[9] Without mutualisation and reciprocity, the neo-liberal mantra of 'personalisation' merely serves to underline just how impersonal services based on 'personal choice' have become.

'workfare' and modern failures on poverty

'Workfare', the third component of the coalition's reform, is the most morally problematic one. Certainly the intention of breaking 'welfare dependency' and facilitating work makes both ethical and economic sense. Contrary to Beveridge's intentions, the British welfare system has become too much a ceiling rather than a safety-net. This has contributed (alongside a collapsed economy in some regions) to abject dependency often stretching over three generations, trapping people in poverty who cannot compete with more skilled immigrants whose pay undercuts the minimum wage, or with those prepared to work sporadically and for extremely little. In this manner, the current model has undermined an ethos of work, saving, caring, and honesty.

But it is the moral attitude to unemployment, exclusion and poverty that is most in question. For the neoliberal right the poor are either inevitable sacrifices to market logic, or else they are a bunch of lazy misfits who need to pull themselves together (or both at once). For the statist left they are passive victims of systematic economic injustice who should be given guilt-ridden and often patronising handouts. In neither case are the poor seen primarily as social actors and continued participants in community.

In reality, however, 'the poor' are subject to the same vagaries of fortune and failure (theirs or others) as all human beings – only in their case to an extreme degree. The outcome of fortune is always a compound of structural circumstance, inheritance of wealth and talent, plus the exercise of effort and virtue. Those who are *un*fortunate remain part of us: they are our neighbours, and so they need to be included within local society. That means helping them in every way possible, both to meet their needs and to develop their ability to help themselves. In turn, poorer people may be expected to make what contribution to the community they can, because to ask for this is precisely *to respect* their continued dignity as human beings.

How does 'Workfare' look in the light of these principles of mutuality and reciprocity? The answer is at best ambivalent. For insisting on some time spent on work and training as a condition of receiving benefit (roughly what is proposed by the coalition government) could mean including the poor in local structures of reciprocity, rather than marginalising them – whether as mere victims or as supposed social parasites. It could mean that the unemployed and their communities try to think out between them new creative tasks that the unemployed might usefully help with, e.g. caring in the community, working in schools or protecting the environment. Such involvement would assist the unemployed to return to the habit of work and begin to equip them with skills, besides giving them some sense of belonging and social worth that often is too little attached even to paid labour.

One insufficiently discussed aspect of the new proposals is their intention to increase the interpersonal factor and the proactive role played by front-line administrators. The problem with 'Workfare' is much the same problem as that of the Universal Credit – everything is filtered through the narrow portal of centralisation, and viewed through the patronising lens of the social engineer. Neither simplification of benefits nor making good use of millions of idle citizens is in itself a bad idea, but the framework in which each is delivered is hopelessly broken and inadequate. The needs of benefit recipients vary widely in type and extent, with many receiving help they don't need, and many more lacking the kind of help they *do* need. The Universal Credit fails to answer these problems, yet the massive variety of benefits creates confusion and fraud, and further traps people in the web of endless bureaucracy. There is a third way, however: the central government should pay a universal credit – but local government should distribute it, and add extra as it sees fit (in consultation with voluntary associations).

The Labour Party and others are correct to say that 'Workfare' will not lead to higher employment and lower dependency if there are not enough jobs available, as the nascent recovery is even more 'job-less' (or generative of pseudo-jobs) than previous economic upturns. All the same, we need again to overcome both a reactive, palliative approach and also a neoliberal view that it is merely 'up to individuals' and their own 'personal choice'. Instead, local *co-operation* can lead to the creation of new enterprises, and government policies and legal-financial structures need to favour such developments. We need to empower local authorities and actors – that is, precisely those people who know and work with those we want to help – to make decisions at that crucial interpersonal level. 'Workfare' will only work best if local people are directed to meet local needs, getting people to build and improve things that they would benefit from and even own – rather than being handed into virtual indenture.

At present, 'Workfare' is still too much a continuation of a centralised attempt to discipline and corral the poor as though they were social lepers. This process of 'confinement' reached its acme with the Victorian workhouse, but has been going on ever since Henry VIII – faced with a massive increase in 'vagabondage' following agricultural enclosures – seized control of parish structures from the power of localities and voluntary fraternities. The task that arises from this long history of centralisation is as daunting as it is urgent: how, on the one hand, to restore the primacy of locality and reciprocity and how, on the other, to deal fairly with people who, at least for now, are likely to remain on the move in an increasingly fluid world?

Once again the alternative to statist and free-market models is a Mutual Jobs Fund – governed by a trust (composed of stakeholders), financed in part by central government and in part by local businesses (providing apprenticeships and training) and coordinated by local councils. After six months, unemployment benefit claimants would be offered the choice between taking up a job or having their benefits cut. Evidence from a DWP report about the Future Jobs Funds (set up in 2009 to help the long-term unemployed back into work) suggests that there are clear individual and social benefits, ranging from much higher chances of being in unsubsidised employment to huge savings for the taxpayers.[10] Communities, professional associations and social enterprise should be included in the governance and operation of such a fund. In this manner, offering everyone paid work would replace benefits and ensure that people are treated with respect and dignity.

There is one final and crucial twist in relation to 'Workfare' and poverty. We have argued that money given to the poor must normally require that they give something in return. But if that is so, then this rule must apply all the more to all the rest of us. For if the poor are also us, then *we are also the poor*, at bottom entirely dependent on the bounty of nature and the gifts of other human beings. It follows that the wealthier should *also* receive as reward – in terms of salaries, bonuses and state benefits – only what can be justified in terms of both their needs and their social contribution. If 'Workfare' invokes mutual fairness, then this implies that such a principle should be applied all the way up.

personal, local and participatory: principles and policies of mutualising welfare

There are both economic and ethical arguments for mutualising welfare. Economically, the need for mutualisation that fuses solidarity with subsidiarity will continue to grow. This is linked not only to longer life expectancy (pensions, healthcare, long-term care, etc.) but also to greater interdependence and the socialisation of risk, which means that jobs are more precarious, and profit-making is increasingly divorced from risk-taking. All of which leaves taxpayers to pick up the tab when bubbles burst and booms turn to bust. Ethically, substantive (not just procedural) justice and genuine fairness (i.e. mutual assistance based on personal needs rather than a culture of individual entitlement) involves a proper measure of contribution and rewards. Ultimately, only a more just economy that pays fairer wages and charges fairer prices will reduce the 'something-for-nothing' culture and bind together profit with risk and work with reward.

To cater for the growing need and to restore popular support for public welfare, Britain requires a system that combines the contributory principle with the 'preferential option for the poor', i.e. minimum assistance to all those in need independently of their financial contribution. In turn, a mutualised model will transcend the false choice between nationalisation and privatisation, which avoids a further centralisation of power and concentration of wealth by establishing mutual health and jobs trusts that are governed independently of government – though accountable to its members and to parliament. This could be achieved by reducing the bloated bureaucracy in Whitehall and the centralistic NHS management in favour of regional, local and even 'hyper-local' levels – including the parish and neighbourhoods.

What the proposed reforms by the left and the right over the past 20 years or so fail to address most of all is the need for a personalised, local and participatory system that does not treat welfare as a set of merely economic transactions but embeds recipients in relationships of trust and responsibility, with a better balance of entitlements and obligations. The current crisis – low economic growth and growing needs such as home care or childcare – means that neither the status quo nor rabid rationalisation are viable options. Instead, the only genuine alternative is to renew and extend Attlee's and Beveridge's vision of a 'New Jerusalem' that promised a unified insurance-based social security system based on the twin principles of contribution and reciprocity. Accordingly, entitlements are earned by citizens, whether through work, or by assuming caring responsibilities, or indeed by contributing to the community, the local environment, etc. The counterpart to the contributory principle is the reciprocal right to a subsistence income for qualifying citizens and their families, without any forms of means-testing.

Moreover, mutualist welfare would combine universal entitlement with localised and personalised provision, e.g. by fostering and extending grassroots initiatives like 'Get Together' or 'Southwark Circle' in London that encompass individual, group and state action. Both initiatives reject old schemes such as 'befriending' or uniform benefits in favour of citizens' activity and community-organising supported by local councils. The link between different actors and levels is neither that of formal rights and entitlements nor of monetarised, market relations but rather one of interpersonal relationships of reciprocity. For example, citizens join welfare schemes like social care as active members who shape the service they become part of. In this manner, they are no longer reduced to being mere passive recipients of a 'one-size-fits-all', top-down model. 'Southwark Circle' works on the principle that people's knowledge of their neighbourhood, community and locality is key to designing services. They are delivered by involving civic participation, social enterprise and the local council.

By contrast, state paternalism or private contract delivery cost more to deliver less, and they lock people either into demoralising dependency on the state, or else financially unaffordable dependency on outsourced, private contractors. Civic participation and mutualism costs less and delivers more because it cuts out the 'middle man' – the growing layers of gate-keepers such as professionals, managers and bureaucrats who assess people's eligibility and enforce centrally determined standards and targets.

But since such models require upfront state investment and continuous involvement of the local council, the state is neither eliminated nor simply retrenched. Rather, the vision of civic participation is inextricably intertwined with the decentralisation of the state in accordance with the twin principles of solidarity and subsidiarity. A genuine alternative to the prevailing options must eschew both conservative paternalism and liberal *laissez-faire* in favour of something like an organic pluralism and a radical politics of virtue that blends a hierarchy of values with an equality of participation in the common good.

Moreover, welfare can no longer be fragmented and impersonal. On the contrary, institutions, governments and socio-economic actors at all levels must find a governing concept that binds together all aspects of social security, including unemployment, health, housing, education, and training – a unified, joined-up system based on contributory rewards and reciprocal rights, as we have tried to indicate throughout this essay.

There is a crucial connection to the idea of a 'living wage'. According to joint research by the Resolution Foundation and the Institute for Public Policy Research, paying UK workers a 'living wage' (instead of the minimum wage) would save the Treasury over £2bn a year by boosting income tax receipts and reducing welfare spending.[11] Employers such as KPMG who have voluntarily adopted the living wage for their staff in London say that it can pay for itself by improving employee motivation, performance and retention. By setting an example to all employers, a renewed emphasis on contribution and reciprocity in both work and welfare promotes economic justice, individual virtue and public honour.

Based on the twin principles of contribution and generosity, 'post-liberal' politics therefore proposes ways of reconfiguring welfare away from state paternalism or private contract delivery towards civic participation and community-organising in close cooperation with central government investment and local councils. Beyond security and in the direction of a fuller flourishing, the same emphasis on mutuality can also translate into policies that incentivise the creation of mutualised banks, local credit unions, and community-based investment trusts. At a time of ageing populations and growing needs, both the left and the right must look beyond redistributive policies to asset-based welfare and decentralised models that foster human relationships of communal care and mutual help.

conclusion

In Britain's low-wage and low-growth economy, state welfare is currently compensating for the failure of finance capitalism and props up a system wherein the governing elites do not abide by the standards of honour they demand of everyone else. By contrast, a mutualised social security model would fuse greater economic justice with a renewed emphasis on interpersonal relationships that honours people's deep desire to earn respect and a place in society through family, community, locality, profession, and faith.

Mutualising welfare involves a number of reforms and policies. First, moving from means-testing to an expanded insurance-based system. This would include creating a new healthcare insurance system and transforming the NHS into a mutual trust – run independently of central government and accountable to its members. Second, making work pay by establishing a Mutual Jobs Fund that guarantees a job to all those who are unemployed for six months and that cuts the benefits of those who refuse to work. Third, supporting the creation of locally-based welfare schemes that are personal and participatory and that treat people with dignity by making them members rather than passive benefit recipients or clients of for-profit private service providers.

Welfare reform must be integrated with other policy areas, most all of housing but also promoting fair prices by enabling councils, communities and housing associations to negotiate not just energy and water prices but also rent on behalf of tenants. All of this requires expanding the introduction of the 'living wage' to reduce welfare dependency and break the vicious circle of debt and demoralisation. Welfare provision should include health, employment, housing, and education policy because it is ultimately a joined-up reality – reflecting the true needs of the whole human person.

chapter 10 – references

1. Karl Polanyi, *The Great Transformation: The Political and Economic Origins of Our Time*, (Boston: Beacon Press, 2001 [orig. pub. 1944]).
2. Anthony Giddens, *The Third Way: The Renewal of Social Democracy* (London: Polity, 1998), pp. 111-28.
3. For this account of gift-exchange building on the work of the French anthropologist Marcel Mauss, see (amongst many others) Jacques T. Godbout with Alain Caillé, *The World of the Gift*, trans. Donald Winkler (Montreal/Kingston: McGill-Queen's University Press, 1998).
4. Frank Field, 'This begins the long track back to sanity', *The Guardian* 6 June 2013, http://www.theguardian.com/commentisfree/2013/jun/06/ed-miliband-social-security-speech.
5. Ed Miliband 'A One-Nation Plan for Social Security Reform', 6 June 2013; Jon Cruddas, 'Earning and Belonging', 6 February 2013.
6. House of Commons Work and Pensions Committee, 'Universal Credit Implementation: meeting the needs of vulnerable claimants', http://www.publications.parliament.uk/pa/cm201213/cmselect/cmworpen/576/57602.htm.
7. Frank Field, 'From the cradle to the grave', *New Statesman* 29 November 2012, http://www.newstatesman.com/politics/politics/2012/11/cradle-grave.
8. See the ResPublica report "Making it Mutual", pp. 153-65, http://www.respublica.org.uk/documents/qrz_Making%20It%20Mutual_The%20ownership%20revolution%20that%20Britain%20needs.pdf.
9. See Graham Allen MP, 'Early Intervention: the Next Steps' (http://www.dwp.gov.uk/docs/early-intervention-next-steps.pdf) and 'Early Intervention: Smart Investment, Massive Savings' (https://www.gov.uk/government/uploads/system/uploads/attachment_data/file/61012/earlyintervention-smartinvestment.pdf); Frank Field MP, 'The Foundation Years: preventing poor children becoming poor adults' (http://webarchive.nationalarchives.gov.uk/20110120090128/http:/povertyreview.independent.gov.uk/media/20254/poverty-report.pdf).
10. DWP, 'Impacts and Costs and Benefits of the Future Jobs Fund', Nov. 2012, http://www.gov.uk/government/uploads/system/uploads/attachment_data/file/223120/impacts_costs_benefits_fjf.pdf.
11. See Matthew Pennycook, 'What price a living wage?', May 2012, http://www.resolutionfoundation.org/media/media/downloads/Final_What_Price_a_Living_Wage_1.pdf; cf. IFS Analysis on the 'living wage', August 2010, at http://www.ifs.org.uk/docs/miliband.pdf.

between priests and levites: putting relationship into the heart of the welfare system
Ed Cox

the war on welfare

There are few more controversial topics in the public policy arena at the present time than welfare reform. Barely a week passes without there being some welfare story receiving national and local media attention as the latest 'skivers and scroungers' have their grim lifestyles paraded through tabloids and broadsheets alike as a warning to any would-be 'benefits cheats'. It sits at the fulcrum of debates about austerity, employment, immigration, and housing and it arouses moral, social and economic instincts that in theory – if not in practice – have the potential to carve out clear dividing lines between the political right and left.

In the run up to the June 2013 Spending Review – the process by which government sets its overall budget for a number of years ahead – the main political parties seemed intent on proving to the general public that each could be as tough as the other on tackling social security spending and, in turn, getting tough with the welfare system. The day after Chancellor George Osborne delivered his review to the House of Commons, the *Daily Mail* front page declared with glee: 'The War on Welfare'.

Exactly which elements of social security spending should be constrained – and how to do this – will be exercising the minds of politicians and policy-makers for some time to come as now all mainstream political parties have signed up to the general principle to cap Annually Managed Expenditure (AME) – the part of the public finances from which most benefits are paid. To this extent, it would appear an important Rubicon has been crossed. The task it would seem is no longer to define how generous a nation can be towards those in need, but how mean and exacting it should become.

Of course, these more recent issues are part of long-standing debates about the principles of the welfare system and politicians will argue that their deliberations simply reflect the fact that they are listening to public concern. But with the risk that the current consensus between the public, the media and policy-makers will calcify in its present form, this essay attempts to understand some of the public perceptions that seem to be fuelling current notions of conditionality. Drawing on the parable of the Good Samaritan, it considers a framework within which current conceptions of welfare might be considered, and it then offers some initial thoughts and ideas about a more relational approach to welfare that might give the progressive left a new place to stand and avoid an apparent race to the bottom.

confusion and conditionality in the welfare system: what the public think

Public perceptions of the welfare system lie at the heart of contemporary debate. As suggested above, both politicians and the media tell us that they are merely reflecting public concerns in their policy making and reporting. This assertion is clearly not as one-directional as it might seem, but assuming it were true, IPPR recently commissioned a YouGov survey to explore what the public understood by welfare and the conditions by which social security benefits can and should be distributed.

In the survey we found that there was a poor understanding of who receives welfare benefits and how these are currently distributed. The public massively underestimates the amount spent on pensioners and substantially overestimates the amount spent on out-of-work benefits for the working age population. Respondents to our poll thought that 20% of the welfare budget goes to retired people and that an equal share is spent on out of work benefits. In fact, a little under half of expenditure (46%) is accounted for by pensioner benefits while just over one tenth (11%) goes on the main benefits for people out of work.

There is a similar amount of confusion about what causes people to need welfare. Our survey explored this by asking respondents to explain recent rises in the welfare budget. When asked to pick two options from a list of potential causes of higher spending, 39% say they think that greater numbers of immigrants coming to Britain is to blame while 30% say rising numbers of people choosing not to work is a key factor. By contrast, 37% pinpoint rising unemployment and falling wages caused by the recession and 34% identify more people in retirement and living longer as a main reason for growth in social security expenditure. As with austerity, the issue of 'blame' for higher welfare spending is deeply contentious.

This confusion about the extent of the welfare system and the causes of need or demand has significant consequences, not least in suggesting that the public perceives it is only a minority who are set to gain from the welfare system and that somehow the system is 'not about me'. Even at the most simple level this perception needs to be reviewed: whether or not any of us suffers the misfortune of being out of work for a time, most of us intend to live to retirement age. Our attitude to the welfare system clearly has implications for us all.

Ideas about who should receive welfare and the reasons for their need have strong links to public attitudes about entitlement and conditionality. Our survey showed that pensioners, disabled people and (to a much lesser extent) the recently unemployed are judged the most deserving of support. Given three choices from a range of options, over three-quarters (76%) of respondents to our poll said that pensioners who have worked most or all of their life are among the most deserving while over two-thirds (67%) put people with a serious, long-term disability in that camp. The next most deserving people are thought to be those who have been in work but just lost their job (39%).

Those 'not trying hard enough to find work', wealthy pensioners and large workless families garner the least public sympathy. Nearly three-quarters (74 per cent) of respondents picked those who could work but aren't making enough effort to do so as among the least deserving of support from the welfare system. Almost two-thirds (63 per cent) put wealthy pensioners with other sources of income in this category, while a little under half (46 per cent) selected families with more than three children and no adult in work.

It is only a small leap from ideas about entitlement to considerations about conditionality and, more particularly, that the welfare system should be based on whether or not an individual has contributed in some way before they can then take something back.

Our survey showed that there is strong consensus that the system does too little for people who have contributed and is too soft on people who could work but don't. Nearly eight in 10 (78%) agree with the former proposition while over three-quarters (76%) back the latter. Far from this being considered a right-wing view, this is held to be true by people of different political perspectives. Large majorities of Labour voters are part of this consensus, with 75% and 65% respectively lining up behind these views.

entitlement and conditionality

Our survey is simply the latest snapshot in a rich literature dating back many centuries as to who does and does not deserve the support of their fellow human beings and the extent to which such support can and should be afforded by the state. From Locke and Burke to Rawls and Sandel, political philosophers and theorists have attempted to prescribe the conditions in which the state might act to promote or inhibit social solidarity. But these issues are considered by even more ancient texts which have the virtue of cutting through the semantics of contemporary academia.

The Parable of the Good Samaritan, a story that appears exclusively in the Gospel of Luke, presents a useful framework with which to consider the contemporary debate. According to the story, told by Jesus to an inquisitive lawyer (for this you could read political philosopher), a man was travelling on the road to Jericho when he was robbed and beaten. First a priest and then a Levite chose to ignore the man's distress but finally a Samaritan (a foreigner) came to his aid and made sure he received the care he needed to recuperate.

On a simple level, one might ask what conditions were being applied by the priest and the Levite that made the victim unworthy of welfare. By contrast, what was it that prompted the Samaritan to stop and make provision for the victim's social security? The beauty of any parable is that much is left to the imagination of the hearer, but allow me to suggest the following.

The priest applied a moral conditionality. He made a judgement about the victim's moral standing and considered him unworthy of his support. The fact that he was travelling along the notoriously dangerous Jericho Road might suggest that he was somehow unworthy: a lone traveller, a travelling salesman, an economic migrant looking for work. Each of these would present grounds for the priest's sense of moral superiority and the priest may too have feared for his own status and safety were he to be seen to care. And so he walked on by.

The Levite – used to characterise a bureaucratic figure in the Jerusalem Temple – applied more of a legal conditionality. Whilst again concerned for his own status, his reason for passing by could be assumed to be on the basis that the victim had not somehow fulfilled his responsibilities or paid his tithes to the temple and to that extent was not deserving of the Levite's support. He somehow failed to fulfil the eligibility criteria and was therefore deemed unsuitable for support.

In each case in this ancient story we can see portents of the contemporary debate. Images in newspapers of large families claiming tens of thousands of pounds in benefits are designed to encourage feelings of moral concern. Lazy suggestions that there might be some kind of link between convicted criminals such as Mick Philpott and families with a 'benefits lifestyle' are deliberately made to provoke moral outrage. And all of this would lay the foundations for a moral conditionality within the benefits system that would allow the state to overlook those who somehow fail to reach the lofty standards of the media, the political class and public opinion polls – clearly the preferred option for much of the political right.

But whilst considerably more sophisticated, the kind of bureaucratic conditionality preferred by the political left is not too distant from the position taken by the Levite, again fearful of the damage that could be done by appearing too caring. Very few 'universal benefits' remain within the present regime and instead we have a social security system which involves sophisticated means testing, including measuring individuals' capability for work, and the application of a wide range of other criteria all of which involve carefully calculated decisions about the worthiness of the recipient and the cost to the Exchequer of any given parameters.

So what of the Samaritan? Three things are striking about his role in the story. First, as a foreigner he would appear to have some form of empathy with the victim that has been robbed; second, he is prepared to risk his own situation by stopping; and third, he makes a financial contribution to the innkeeper who assists in the victim's recuperation. Rather than imposing some kind of moral or bureaucratic conditionality upon his assistance, his support could perhaps be characterised as empathetic entitlement.

Little in the contemporary debate would appear to be pulling in this direction. There are some political theorists who argue for a guaranteed minimum income or some other form of basic entitlement as 'the social bases of democratic participation and inclusion' but they are few and far between.[1] Even Rawls would appear to argue that 'justice' and citizenship are based on some form of contributory principle rather than personal desert.[2] Perhaps the closest one comes to a notion of empathetic entitlement is in the emerging literature on the relational state.

In a recent publication on the subject, a range of contributors set out the weaknesses of the market and the target-driven approach to public service reform often known as New Public Management (NPM) – very much a bureaucratic model of state action.[3] Despite improving standards in many aspects of public service, advocates of a more relational state emphasise the need for human relationships to be given greater priority as a goal of public policy. They acknowledge the limits of state power in advancing social solidarity; and they advocate the redistribution of power in more localised and collective forms.

The final section of this contribution will attempt to explore what empathetic entitlement and a more relational approach to welfare might mean in practice.

the three C's of relational welfare

Whether on moral, financial or legalistic grounds, the debate on welfare has become increasingly narrow, mean and divisive. Relational welfare – founded upon a deeper and more conscious understanding of our own needs and the needs of those around us, born out of everyday relationships – presents an opportunity to reclaim a progressive narrative for a welfare system that is compassionate, inclusive and majoritarian. To achieve this, though, a more relational approach needs to be underpinned by three clear principles: contribution, clarity and co-operation.

The contributory principle is often cited as being part of the so-called 'Beveridge principles' associated with the post-war welfare state whereby unemployment and sickness benefits were paid in respect of contributions made through taxation and national insurance. Over recent decades there has been a steady decline in the role of contributions in the working age welfare system, in part because means testing has been seen to be more affordable and, in some cases, out of a desire to be inclusive and universal.

In recent times, there has been something of a resurgence in interest in the contributory principle, largely as there is a perception that means testing has led to perverse incentives in the system and to disincentivised responsible behaviour. But the argument for a contributory principle within a relational welfare system is not a moral or legal one. Rather, it is to create the basis upon which a more empathetic or neighbourly system can flourish.

It is interesting to consider that pensioners are judged the most deserving of welfare payments and this is the one area of the welfare system that has retained a reasonably strong contributory principle. It could be argued that this is not as simple as the public believing that pensioners should get back what they have paid in, but also that there is significant social solidarity with older people as the vast majority of us will ultimately become one.

The question, then, is how to establish a similar solidarity and empathy in other aspects of welfare. While Universal Credit could provide a limited form of 'social assistance' unrelated to prior contributions, we need to conceive of other forms of social insurance which are clearly linked to a set of life events that affect many working people such as losing a job, having a baby, or having an illness or accident, paid for directly through 'national insurance'. Child Benefit could be front loaded to tie-in more directly with maternity and paternity leave rather than being perceived as long-term reward for having a large family, with a higher rate or lump sum being paid in a child's early years but less as the child gets older. At other stages of life, a 'caring entitlement' could be paid to enable someone to take time out of the labour market to care for a sick or elderly relative. And much more could be done to acknowledge and fund the importance of personal support, relationships and networks in successful job-seeking, perhaps to support work experience opportunities. This could be combined with greater guarantees for learning and work for young people, though with greater obligations to make up for a lack of contributions at an early stage in their careers.

Linking welfare payments much more directly to the real life experiences we all share must sit at the heart of a successful contributory system. But to build such empathy there is a need for clarity.

Clarity can be achieved, first and foremost, by avoiding lazy generalisations about a wide range of different benefits and services distributed for a wide variety of reasons. Judging the entire 'welfare bill' on the behaviour of a small group of dysfunctional families is about as meaningful as judging 'the health bill' on the performance of a small group of maverick GPs. As set out above, a more relational system needs to link welfare payments more directly and discreetly with life cycle events. One of the biggest claims of Universal Credit is the desire to simplify the benefits system, but there is a danger that an over-simplified system will do almost the opposite and become nothing more than a means-tested carrot – or more likely stick – with little link between need and payment. Perhaps we would do well not to talk about 'welfare' at all?

Another way in which clarity can be achieved is through a more local system. One of the greatest sources of antipathy with the current system is that it appears that national benefits rules drive perverse incentives in particular places. This is especially true in relation to housing benefits where in some neighbourhoods they can appear too mean and in others too generous. It may not be right to localise every benefit but having housing and employment benefits that are more closely related to local housing and labour markets might also build greater understanding and solidarity within the welfare system.

Perhaps the most important change that is needed to improve clarity is to ensure that the structural causes of hardship are driven out of the system rather than subsidised by it. Martin Luther King said in 1967 that "we are called to play the Good Samaritan on life's roadside, but that will only be an initial act. One day we must come to see that the whole Jericho Road must be transformed so that men and women will not be constantly beaten and robbed as they make their journey on life's history."[4]

So, for example, it cannot be right that the welfare system is subsidising high private rents through housing benefits – we need to build more houses. It cannot be right that the Winter Fuel Allowance is subsidising extortionate energy costs or that Tax Credits are underpinning a low wage economy. A relational welfare system requires action on the causes of the market failures that lead to so much of the growing demand. This requires wider action in all areas of public policy, but it also requires co-operation.

A welfare system that depends too greatly on state action will inevitably diminish social solidarity and bring increasing cost pressures to bear on the Exchequer. It must always be recognised that the majority of caring, nurture and support takes place informally in the context of families and communities, and this needs constant affirmation and support.

This is not to say that the state should not be a major player, but that it should not be *the sole* player. Just as for a wide range of public services, there is a growing recognition that the so-called co-productive capacities of individuals and communities are necessary to drive efficiency and effectiveness, this is also true with welfare, especially in relation to employment and active labour market policies.

There is increasing recognition of the importance of more tailored support for job seekers – particularly for those furthest from the labour market – in the form of a named individual support worker who can address the multiple or complex needs of an individual. But also that strengthening a job seeker's own networks, communities and wider social capital is fundamental to them being ready and able to find decent work. The co-operation between statutory providers and communities – often brokered through local voluntary organisations – must also be complemented by businesses. Incentives for all employers to achieve social as well as economic goals should also be within the scope of a more relational state and a means of tackling the low-wage-no-wage cycle that affects too many people.

conclusion

The 'War on Welfare', driven by the complex relationships between the media, politics and public opinion, is increasingly a race to the bottom. Whilst it may bring the odd beggar or protester to Downing Street or Fleet Street, it is on the Jericho Roads and housing estates of our provincial towns and cities where its impact is proving to be the most acute. And there are thousands of Good Samaritans already playing their part.

The concept of relational welfare attempts to capture a more optimistic and empathetic spirit, a more genuine sense that 'we are all in this together'. Whilst there might always be a place for some forms of more universal, social assistance, as part of the drive to create a wider relational state, we need to bring clarity to the ways in which 'benefits' are understood. We need to link the whole system to the life experiences we all share. We need an understanding of conditionality and contribution that doesn't dwell exclusively on a moral or legal prerogative but on a sense of empathy and understanding with those in need. And above all else, we need a system – part of a wider relational state – which tackles the reasons for our needs at their root. Only then will the Jericho Road become an occasional diversion between life's more wonderful highways of hope.

chapter 11 – references

1. King D., *Making People Work: democratic consequences of welfare* in Mead L. and Beem C. (eds.) Welfare Reform and Political Theory (Russell Sage Foundation, 2005).

2. Mead L. and Beem C. (eds.), *Welfare Reform and Political Theory* (Russell Sage Foundation, 2005).

3. Cooke G. and Muir R., *The relational state: how recognising the importance of human relationships could revolutionise the role of the state* (IPPR, 2012).

4. Martin Luther King Jr "A time to break the silence" quoted in Hicks D. and Valeri M., *Global Neighbours* (Eerdmans, 2008).

12

welfare and moral community
Nick Spencer

attitudes to 'welfare'

Although the term 'welfare state' has been in use now for around three-quarters of a century, it has described subtly different entities over that time. When the term was first coined, in the pre-war period, it was used to denote a state that ruled *for* the people, in contrast to the 'Power State', which ruled *over* them. In the years after the war the phrase came, in Britain, to denote a system, based on William Beveridge's war-time report and implemented by the Attlee government, in which (for the most part) flat rate, universal, mandatory social insurance provided a social safety net through which no-one could, in theory, fall.

The same phrase is still used today in spite of the fact that the system we describe is unrecognisably different from that of 1945. In the words of the Institute for Fiscal Studies, "very little of today's welfare system bears even a passing resemblance to the system envisaged in the Beveridge Report."[1] This is partly because the shape, size and expectations of the population it serves have changed out of all recognition,[2] but it is also because the size, mechanics and fundamental purpose of the system itself has also changed, the insurance-based system that once formed backbone of the Attlee settlement now reduced to a vestigial stump.

Public opinion has also changed, although more subtly, over time. In the late 1940s, there was widespread, nearly unqualified approval of the welfare state. Similarly, according to various research studies today, conducted for/ by British Social Attitudes,[3] *Prospect*/ YouGov,[4] and BBC/ComRes, the *original* concept of the welfare state remains highly popular. Only one in ten people disagrees that the creation of the welfare state is 'one of Britain's proudest achievements'.

However, public attitudes to its *present operation* are more sceptical, with a growing proportion of the population associating today's welfare state with unfairness, inefficiency and dependency. The context of this change is important. Over the last 30 years, the public has tended to be more sympathetic to increased welfare spending, and to benefit recipients themselves, during periods of economic downturn – and vice versa.[5] This makes intuitive sense. During recessions, people need more help, feel more vulnerable, and know more people who are on benefits, thereby drawing the stigma that is often attached to welfare. During times of plenty, the opposite is true.

Research over recent years has shown that this inverse correlation – between security/wealth and attitudes to welfare – is becoming decoupled, and public opinion about universal, state-based welfare provision is much more reserved than it once was, *inspite* of the deepest and longest recession in the post-war period. Thus, for example, in 2010, three in ten respondents recommended an increase in taxation and spending compared with five in 10 who did so in 2002. Similarly, whereas 20 years ago (at the end of another recession), only 26% of people agreed or agreed strongly that "if welfare benefits weren't so generous, people would learn to stand on their own two feet," today 54% do. Although the most recent data from British Social Attitudes survey for 2012 indicate a slight reverse in recent trends, the direction of travel over the last generation is reasonably clear.[6] We are falling out of love with the welfare state.

two caveats

It would be easy simply to wring our hands at such data and bemoan how individualistic and mean-spirited the British public has become. That, indeed, is how some commentators have reacted, blaming public ignorance, lurid media tales of benefit fraud and the ghost of Margaret Thatcher for the shifting opinion. No doubt all three factors are involved in some way, but to blame the public for not being as positive about the role of the state in welfare provision as it apparently should be is not only rather haughty but, more importantly, is to miss critical nuances that change the picture. Two in particular are worth noting.

The first is that the public's reaction against state-based welfare provision is not undifferentiated. Whatever the overall direction of travel is, support for state spending on health and disability remains high and constant. When asked whether they think it should be the government's responsibility to provide health care for the sick, 83% of people said it definitely should be in 2012 (compared with 85% in 1990). Similarly, in 2010, 85% of people said they thought the government "should mainly be responsible for ensuring that people have enough to live on if they become sick for a long time or disabled", compared with 7% who thought it should be mainly a person's employer, and 7% who thought it should be mainly the person themselves and their family. However sceptical we are becoming about state-based welfare provision, it is not about its use to cover sickness and disability.

The second caveat is that the public's reaction against *state-based* welfare provision is not the same as a reaction against welfare. Put another way, for all that public opinion has swung against the state as the primary source and provider of 'welfare' in some areas, it has not embraced thoroughgoing individualism as the obvious alternative. Thus, the percentage of people who believe that a person's employer is mainly responsible for ensuring "that people have enough money to live on in retirement" rose from 7.4% in 2001 to 11.2% in 2010. The percentage who thought that the person themselves or their family (the two options are rolled into one in the BSA questionnaire) had the same responsibility rose from 29% to 35% over the same time. Similarly, when asked in 2012, who they thought should be responsible for reducing child poverty in Britain, 78% said central government (up from 74% in 2009) and 62% said local government (vs. 55% in 2009), whilst at the same time 30% said friends/relatives of people in poverty (vs. 26% in 2009) and 28% said charities (vs. 23% in 2009).[7]

These two observations make it clear that the public's turn against state welfare is neither a blanket one nor does it constitute an uncomplicated embrace of hard-nosed individualism. Instead, the reaction is concentrated in a number of specific areas. Thus, the public is more sceptical about state welfare support for parents on standard rate tax receiving Child Benefit, for the low paid who are receiving support through benefits, and for single parents. The public is also considerably more hostile to the government taking responsibility for ensuring that people have enough to live on if they become unemployed.

There are pertinent questions here about whether the public's increased emphasis on the responsibility of employers, families and voluntary organisations to meet people's needs is matched by their own behaviour. The percentage of people who told British Social Attitudes that they were a member of a voluntary group that helped the sick, elderly, children, or another vulnerable group actually fell slightly (from 1.9% to 1.5%) between 1997 and 2012. Similarly, the percentage of people who say they are a member of another "local community or voluntary group" (i.e. one that does not have a function like those above) has remained static, at 6.7%, over the last twenty years. Increased support for localised welfare activity does not necessarily translate into increased local welfare activity.

Nevertheless, the fact remains that it is not simply that the public are necessarily more heartless than they were a generation ago concerning those in need, but rather that they see the responsibility for care shifting away from the individual as taxpayer and towards the individual as employer, employee, volunteer or family member.

a sense of 'us'

The reasons for this are many and complex. One is wealth: a wealthy population feels less need for state-based welfare support than a poorer one. A second is institutional trust, or the lack of it: trust in politics (and institutions generally) is dismally low, and people seem not to feel their money is being administered well, fairly or to people who genuinely deserve it.

More significant than either of those, however (at least for the purposes of this essay) is the question of common identity and responsibility. Do I have a meaningful sense of belonging? If so, to whom and to what extent? How 'thick' is that sense? And how exacting are its responsibilities? It is our answers to these questions that determine the welfare landscape we cultivate.

It was precisely an overpowering *national* sense of 'us' that enabled the creation of the welfare state in the first instance. A nation that had pooled its resources and energies as never before to come through the greatest external threat in its history was a nation acutely conscious of a sense of 'us'. That sense was not simply negative and circumstantial, forged entirely in opposition to a deadly foe. It was positive also, drawing on a powerful common identity – the 'Christian civilisation' that Churchill and many others spoke about – which it transmuted into a common peacetime object, namely a nationalised system of mutual social protection secured by insurance. A strong national sense of 'us' was called on to win the peace, as it had been to win the war.

Two important factors have changed since this happened, however. The first relates to the nation. Few prominent British politicians would now describe contemporary Britain as the hope for Christian civilisation. The sense of national destiny and responsibility that was once pervasive is gone, as is any substantive notion even of national identity (witness the repeated attempts to define Britishness over the last 15 years). Large scale net inward migration; the evaporation of a normative Christian moral atmosphere, however faintly it was once felt; and the now-instinctive mistrust of authority and government – all these have combined to erode still further that overpowering sense of mutual responsibility that underpinned the Attlee settlement. The nationalised sense of 'us', that founded and sustained the welfare state, is much weakened.

The second factor relates to the system itself. The Attlee settlement was an insurance system, predicated largely on flat rate contributions. In other words, the principal bond of unity, the centre of ethical gravity of the whole system, was *just desert*: the longer you worked or the more you paid in, the more you would (probably) receive, and vice versa.

Over the years, this original system was reshaped, contribution giving way to general taxation, flat rate contribution to progressive rates, and receipt according to contribution to receipt according to means testing. In other words, the centre of gravity shifted from *just desert* to *perceived need*, the primary call on the common purse being not whether someone had worked and saved, but whether they were in need.

Need-centred systems *can* function perfectly successfully, but in order to do so they require a very thick sense of identity to sustain them. The reason for this is twofold. First, a need-centred system inherently fails to value, and therefore ends up disincentivising, industriousness. In such a system, you don't get more out the more you put in, which invites the question (however quietly asked), why bother putting much in. Second, a need-centred system pays particular regard to, indeed prioritises, vulnerability, and therefore ends up incentivising dependency. In such a system, the needier you are, the greater call you have on the common purse, which invites the temptation (however quietly acknowledged) to exaggerate your needs.

In order to overcome such dynamics, a need-centred system relies on a very strong bond of mutual trust and responsibility. It requires participants to maintain necessary levels of personal diligence (i.e. work and saving) even though they know they will probably not benefit from them. It requires them not to exaggerate their level of need, even though they would probably benefit from doing so. And it requires them to trust one another in all this – not only to maintain their levels of work and to be honest about their need, but to trust that others are also being so. In short, it requires sufficient and sustained virtues of diligence, honesty and trust to nullify or overcome the free-rider problem.

It is important to stress that those who shifted the system in the direction of being need-centred were not intentionally disincentivising hard work or incentivising need. To imagine they were would be unduly cynical. Indeed, it is possible to see the development of such a system of mutual responsibility as an example of the highest, rather than lowest, moral aspiration. Such a system calls on a people to care and serve for those who most need care and service, and not to count the cost in doing so.

In this regard, such a need-centred system was a (perhaps unconscious) adaptation of the New Testament ethic in which "all the believers were together and had everything in common. They sold property and possessions to give to *anyone who had need*."[8] The emphasis in the public ministry of the early church was that it was need that dictated generosity. Such was an ethic founded on the example and teaching of Christ, such as in the Good Samaritan, in which it is the solely the need of the victim that commanded a practical response – and where ethnic, cultural, and religious differences, not to mention personal cost and risk, were immaterial. A need-centred social system is the highest calling but also, therefore, the most demanding.

responsibilities

Certain elements of the post-war welfare state, in its fullest sense, show how this vision of a need-centred community could work. And not just 'could': the ongoing public support for the NHS shows how it continues to do so. Those who have paid very little in taxes, such as children and the young, are treated by the health service simply on account of their need. Those who have not paid enough, such as the long-term unemployed or the chronically ill, similarly get the service they need. The system is funded by those who have for the sake of those who need.[9] Merit does not come into the equation.

The NHS, and affiliated services connected with disability, increasingly seem to be the exception, however. (And even here the edges are being frayed, with questions being – legitimately – raised about the extent to which new residents or, for example, persistent smokers can draw on a need-centred system.) Beyond the NHS, the ingredients to sustain a need-centred system are simply not present in the public conscience.

The reason for this may be glimpsed in a second, rather more unsettling incident from the life of the early church. In Acts chapter 5, a couple called Ananias and Saphira donate the money from property they have sold to the common purse, but in doing so disingenuously withhold some of the proceeds. This emerges and the apostle Peter severely berates the couple, not for their lack of generosity but their deception. This short and disturbing vignette – both Ananias and Saphira keel over and die when exposed – serves as a counterpoint to the earlier story of how the needs-based community flourished. That first account talked about how "all the *believers* were together and had everything in common" (emphases added). In other words, there was a common existential and ethical bond the underpinned the community, and which enabled it to serve "*anyone* who had need". Once that is undermined, the capacity to sustain a need-centred system is damaged. Ananias and Saphira were not free-riders as such. They did not claim what was not rightly theirs. But they betray the bonds of trust and honesty on which the community's identity, and its ability to answer need, depended.

Post-war Britain is rather different from the early church, but the parallel is a meaningful one. The story of Britain's post-war welfare settlement is one of how the nation gradually, almost accidentally, developed a needs-centred welfare system, which demanded the strongest possible sense of mutual identity, trust and responsibility, just as the nation itself felt its sense of national identity, mutual trust, and unqualified responsibility to one another attenuate.

conclusion

How might we respond to this? Three responses present themselves. The first is to throw in the towel, and adopt the essentially libertarian response of dismantling state-based welfare altogether in favour of a society of self-interest. The second is the mirror opposite, namely to soldier on without paying attention to the new public landscape.

The first is unappealing: not only morally problematic but clearly not where the public is or wants to go. The second is unrealistic: carrying on with business-as-usual is positively Canute-like, not so much in commanding the incoming waters to stop as ordering the withdrawing tide of public opinion to return to where it was three generations ago.

There is a third option. This is to pay more serious attention to what public opinion is saying about a greater variety of welfare provision. Doing so might suggest several points of action, three of which may be mentioned in the space available.

First, we need to make a powerful case for those parts of the nationalised need-based system that remain, particularly health. Nigel Lawson once remarked that the NHS was the closest thing that the English had to a religion. Perhaps so, but the English (or indeed the British) are as capable of losing their medical religion as their Christian one, and we cannot assume that public support will remain as high and steady as it has for the last generation, especially when the irresistible force of ever greater medical needs meets the immovable object of a limited budget. In such a clash, the *moral* case for a health system whose fundamental criterion for access is need must be made repeatedly.

Second, those aspects of the welfare state, such as social security, where a need-centred system is witnessing the melancholy, long, withdrawing roar of public support need reform, specifically reform into the kind of system that a 21st century population *can* support. This, in effect, means change into a system centred on desert – the insurance-based system that once was – rather than need.

This could be a costly reform, not only financially, but also potentially socially. Britain in 2013 is not Britain in 1945. The social fabric is more threadbare with many bigger holes – fragmented families and communities – and the move from a need-centred system of means-tested welfare to a desert-centred system based on insurance risks people falling through those holes. This eventuality cannot be ignored or minimised, which is why the second response necessitates a third, namely to enable a much greater role in welfare for those groups that are need-centred, namely voluntary, charitable and church groups. Shifting from a need-centred system will seem just too costly to those most in need of help unless other means of support are encouraged and maintained. William Beveridge understood well that his proposed system required a secure foundation of voluntary (and indeed mutual) activity on which to rest. In this, as in so much else, he was prophetic. Ultimately reform of the welfare state will succeed only if we can re-form the welfare society in which it operates.

chapter 12 – references

1. http://www.ifs.org.uk/publications/6475.
2. Beveridge's proposals "were for a country in which, for the most part, men worked and married women didn't, the only lone parents were widows, and life expectancy was lower than the pension age… At the time of the report less than 1 in 20 births was outside marriage; today more than 1 in 5 children grow up in a lone parent household. Male life expectancy has climbed from around 63 in 1940 to 78 in 2010." See http://www.ifs.org.uk/publications/6475.
3. Clery, Elizabeth (2012), 'Are tough times affecting attitudes to welfare? in Park, A., Clery, E., Curtice, J., Phillips, M. and Utting, D. (eds.) (2012), British Social Attitudes: the 29th Report, London: NatCen Social Research, p. 12.
4. See Peter Kellner, 'A quiet revolution', Prospect, March 2012: http://www.prospectmagazine.co.uk/magazine/a-quiet-revolution-britain-turns-against-welfare/.
5. Taylor-Gooby, P. (2004), 'The work-centred welfare state', in Park, A., Curtice, J., Thomson, K., Bromley, C. and Phillips, M. (eds.), British Social Attitudes: the 21st Report, London: Sage.
6. "Data for 2012 may indicate a break in the long-term trend, although it should be noted that similar shifts in opinion in recent years have proved temporary." 'Government spending and welfare: Changing attitudes towards the role of the state', in Alison Park et al British Social Attitudes: the 30th Report (London, 2013), p. 46.
7. This was a multi-code question, i.e. respondents were not required to choose between options, which is why the total of responses exceeds 100%. For reference, 42% said the people in poverty themselves (vs. 40% in 2009).
8. Acts 2.44-45; emphases added.
9. One might argue that this is simply enlightened self-interest: people know that they will one day require health treatment (when they get old) and indeed may require costly health treatment much earlier (if they fall chronically ill). However, were this the only motivating factor, an increasingly wealthy society would simply withdraw support for the NHS in favour of a personalised health insurance system. Moreover, similar arguments about employment (I may one day be unemployed; I feel more vulnerable to unemployment in a recession) have conspicuously failed to shore up public support for unemployment benefit and its recipients over the last decade.

afterword
Matthew Taylor

If this fascinating collection of essays were to be a foreigner's first introduction to the UK welfare state they might end up somewhat bemused. On the one hand, many of the essays recognise that the issues of welfare and its reform are contentious to the point of toxicity. On the other, there seems – at least superficially – to be remarkable consensus about what needs to change. "Surely most of you agree?" our visitor might exclaim. "What you want is a system which achieves three things: first, to put a brake on spiralling and unsustainable costs; second, to better target resources on those in most genuine need; and third, to provide incentives and rewards for benign social behaviours such as working, caring and saving?"

But these three goals – managing costs, helping the most needy and providing incentives – will be immediately recognisable to any student of public policy as the classic welfare 'trilemma' – you can have any two but it is simply impossible to achieve all three. Indeed, because it is not acceptable to abandon entirely any of these commendable goals, current policy tries and fails to meet all three, while public attitude about which should be given priority ebbs and flows. Meanwhile, social advances (increasing life expectancy) and economic problems (unemployment and stagnant living standards) conspire to make the 'trilemma' ever more intractable.

It is a reflection both of current public opinion and the theological bent of these essays that there is a recurrent emphasis on the degree to which the welfare state encourages, or more often allegedly discourages, moral behaviour (although it is worth noting in passing the general lack of conclusive evidence for the disincentive effects of benefits on the motivation of the unemployed or under-employed). But while there are authors who are to be commended for identifying where money could be saved in order to strengthen incentives and reciprocity, there is sometimes what appears to be a lack of realism about the nature of practical reform.

For example, many authors support the enhancement of conditionality in the system with a promise of meaningful remunerated work or structured volunteering balanced by the threat of a loss of benefits for those who don't take up this 'offer'. The implication is not only that this will make the system fairer and more robust but that it might also save money. However, there is less recognition of the existing scale of what is euphemistically called 'sanctioning' (580,000 withdrawals of benefit between October 2012 and June 2103), of the substantial cost of the offer that goes with conditionality (whether that is subsiding jobs or volunteer placements), and of the simple fact that people who fall below the level of basic subsistence often end up costing the state more, for example, in the demands that the truly destitute place on public services. Reciprocal conditionality might help with incentives but it probably doesn't help with costs.

There are what might be called 'middle ground' ideas in this collection – forms of structural change which lie between idealist principles and detailed reforms. But again – to be critical – the idea, for example, that mutualising or localising welfare in any significant way solves the 'trilemma' seems to be a triumph of hope over calculation.

It is not that these or any other ideas in these pages are without merit – far from it; the problem is more the absence of a model of change to carry us from the failings of the present system to the sunny uplands of a re-moralised welfare state, a model that is credible in both policy and political terms. Having volunteered to write only an afterword to this collection it may be impertinent of me to offer my own prescription, especially as elements of it are dotted around the collection, but I can perhaps suggest one way of making substantive change more possible.

A significant and broad reform of the welfare system which goes to the heart of the values it represents and reinforces may require three elements. First, a concerted attempt at public education in order that the public – or at least those who care – better understand the kind of difficult trade-offs that are involved in any reform. We won't gain support for difficult change as long as large parts of the public think the only barriers to a fair and effective system are political cowardice, claimant fecklessness or the need for a simple one-off reform, such as abolishing universal Winter Fuel Payments for the affluent elderly. If a step change in public awareness seems unrealistic it is worth recalling how, as part of his successful pension review between 2002 and 2006, Adair Turner pretty quickly achieved a consensus over the initially highly controversial idea of starting to raise the pension entitlement age (a process which almost certainly needs further acceleration).

Second, the debate about welfare must not, as several authors recognise, be restricted to state spending and services but also to wider aspects of our society and economy which generate demands on the state (Ed Miliband's interest in 'pre-distribution' is an example of this thinking). To succeed, a thoroughgoing reform of welfare must be a society-wide project with implications for business, the voluntary sector and communities themselves, and not just one about public policy or the responsibilities of welfare claimants.

Third, any such process almost certainly requires cross-party political buy-in. There will no doubt be short term pain for long term gain, and losers often shout loud while winners stay silent. No party can be expected to be brave if the others see such bravery as an opportunity to make mischief.

In short, we need a new Beveridge. Who on earth would be willing to take on such a task and who could command sufficient political consent and public trust is probably as hard a question as any of the others addressed in this collection. But without at least aiming for a new settlement we will almost certainly be stuck with the continued tinkering (even the jumbo tinkering represented by the Universal Credit) that has made a system designed by so many clever people with so much good intent so manifestly unfit for modern purpose.